Howle

RAISING YOUR GIFTED CHILD

Books by the authors

HOW TO GET YOUR CHILDREN TO DO WHAT YOU WANT
THEM TO DO with Paul Wood, M.D.

HELP YOUR CHILDREN TO BE SELF-CONFIDENT
with John V. Flowers

HOW TO GET YOUR CHILDREN TO BE GOOD STUDENTS/HOW
TO GET YOUR STUDENTS TO BE GOOD CHILDREN
with James Pugh

RAISING YOUR CHILD TO BE A SEXUALLY HEALTHY ADULT
with John V. Flowers and Jennifer Horsman

Books by John V. Flowers

HELP YOUR CHILDREN TO BE SELF-CONFIDENT
with Bernard Schwartz

RAISING YOUR CHILD TO BE A SEXUALLY HEALTHY ADULT
with Jennifer Horsman and Bernard Schwartz

Books by Jennifer Horsman

RAISING YOUR CHILD TO BE A SEXUALLY HEALTHY ADULT
with John V. Flowers and Bernard Schwartz

John V. Flowers
Jennifer Horsman
Bernard Schwartz

RAISING YOUR GIFTED CHILD

PRENTICE-HALL, INC., Englewood Cliffs, N.J. 07632

Raising Your Gifted Child
by John V. Flowers, Jennifer Horsman,
and Bernard Schwartz
©1982 by John V. Flowers,
Jennifer Horsman, and Bernard Schwartz

Address inquiries to Prentice-Hall, Inc.,
Englewood Cliffs, N.J. 07632
Printed in the United States of America
Prentice-Hall International, Inc., London
Prentice-Hall of Australia, Pty. Ltd., Sydney
Prentice-Hall Canada, Inc., Toronto
Prentice-Hall of India Private Ltd., New Delhi
Prentice-Hall of Japan, Inc., Tokyo
Prentice-Hall of Southeast Asia Pte Ltd., Singapore
Whitehall Books Limited, Wellington, New Zealand

10   9   8   7   6   5   4   3   2   1

ISBN 0-13-752766-7 {PBK}

ISBN 0-13-752774-8

Library of Congress Cataloging in Publication Data

Flowers, John V.
    Raising your gifted child.

    Includes index.
    1. Gifted children.   2. Child-rearing—United States.
I. Horsman, Jennifer.   II. Schwartz, Bernard. (date)
III. Title.
HQ773.5.F58 1982   649'.155   82-9066
ISBN 0-13-752774-8   AACR2
ISBN 0-13-752766-7 (pbk.)

Contents

Introduction

The Many Shapes of Giftedness

All children are special, unique individuals. Every child has a distinct, personal way of perceiving and relating to our world, an individual way of just being. And all children display different talents and aptitudes, successes and achievements. In addition to this uniqueness, some children are also gifted.

Giftedness, like children themselves, comes in many shapes and sizes. Most commonly, when we speak of giftedness, it is mental giftedness we are referring to. Mental giftedness is basically a cognitive acceleration from the norm in one's ability to comprehend, analyze, and retain information. Theresa, mother of four, explains how she first recognized this ability in her daughter Lisa:

Lisa, our middle child, at first seemed quite average. She did, however, start speaking very early and I remember once I counted the number of words in one sentence and there were nine words, and she was only two and a half! Then, by the time she was four, she could read independently. My husband and I thought she was just smart. We never knew how smart until she entered kindergarten and the teacher requested that she be tested. We were certainly surprised; we just weren't expecting one of our children to be that gifted.

In addition to mental giftedness, there are several other areas in which children may excel beyond the norm. Another significantly form of giftedness is found in the highly motivated child. These children display a remarkable ability to focus attention and energy in one area or one set of areas. These areas are pursued by the motivated child ardently, passionately, and often to the exclusion of all else life has to offer. Pam described this characteristic in her young son Jason:

Jason was always an intense, quiet child. Where other children would play with toy after toy, tiring of each one, discarding each one as often as they changed clothes, Jason would play with one toy for months at a time. As he got older this pattern of concentrated focus continued. The only other thing he would do was read. He preferred nonfiction to fiction, and I think he went through the entire school library by the time he was eight. But then one day he read one book on astronomy, then another and another until I had to travel to the city's main library to keep keep feeding his interest. He is twelve now and is still pursuing this interest with incredible persistence. He has his own telescope, he is still going through book after book on the subject, and he regularly visits the professors of astronomy at the university.

Motivationally gifted children are likely to be (though certainly are not always) well above average in intelligence. Their ability to focus on and master specific subjects or skills is a most valued asset in our highly specialized society, and they are likely to excel in their chosen areas of interest. At the very least they learn that success or the mastery of any one thing requires hard work and persistence.

Social giftedness is another, often overlooked form of giftedness. Some children display an unusual gift of understanding, compassion, or courage of convictions at early ages. The actions of such children, cloaked in innocence, are sometimes poignant examples of how we should treat fellow human beings. In the following story, one teacher describes such a child:

Carol was the most beautiful, likable, and incredibly outgoing child I have seen in my ten years of teaching kindergarten. Young and old alike were charmed by her. Why, we wouldn't even need a playground monitor with Carol, for she would organize games and insist not only that everyone participate, but that everyone play fair. I would see her quite a few times come to the rescue of other children who were being bullied. One time (I'll never forget it) a mother came to school to hand out her daughter's birthday party invitations. All but two children were invited, and needless to say, the two uninvited children were so hurt they began crying. I must confess, I didn't even know what to do; I just stood by, stunned and angry at the mother's inconsideration. Well, Carol immediately grasped the situation and boldly confronted this mother by saying, "Why didn't you invite them too?" Now, the mother stood stunned and silent. Without waiting for a reply, Carol ran and got scissors, cut her invitation into three parts, and handed the two left-out kids a part!

I called Carol's mother to explain what happened. She laughed and said that Carol was the last of eight children and was indeed very special. She told me that just the other day, they were shopping downtown when Carol noticed an old man, wearing tattered and torn clothes (probably an alcoholic) and begging. Unhesitatingly, Carol approached him and dumped the contents of her small coin purse in his lap. Then she ran back and, with tears in her eyes, asked her mom if he could come to their house for dinner.

I don't know what's going to happen to Carol, what kind of person will emerge from this unusual child. All I know is that the world certainly can use her.

Children who do have this intuitive social sense need their kindness nurtured and their empathy appreciated. And, hopefully, these children will develop and maintain their gift. In any case, we certainly can learn from these very gifted children.

Physical ability is another form of giftedness. Exceptional agility, coordination, and strength, coupled with motivation, can create athletic excellence. Like the highly motivated child, the athletic child learns self-confidence and goal-directed behavior at an early age. Cheryl, a gymnastic instructor, describes one such child:

I met him one day as I was tanning by our apartment pool. I saw him tumbling in the grass and I assumed he was taking lessons somewhere. We started talking and I discovered that he had never had lessons and he learned everything from watching TV. I was impressed. I started teaching him some tricks and before an hour had passed he could do flip-flops! He learned so quickly. I couldn't let a kid like this get away, so I went to his mom and talked her into starting him in lessons at the club where I worked. Within a year, Kevin was in Class One on our team, an accomplishment that usually takes five years!

A final form of giftedness, the one most difficult to define and most frequently discussed, is creativity. Most people think of creativity as being associated with the arts: painting, sculpture, singing, acting, writing, choreography, or interpretation of dance. If one asked one hundred people if they were creative, 90 percent would enthusiastically respond, "Yes!" Are all these people telling the truth? In a sense, yes. We are each unique individuals, different from all others, and because of this we all view the world differently. This leads us to express our views of the world in different and unique ways. Many mothers, such as Sharon, view their children as creative:

Shelly is seven and has quite a bit of artistic creativity. We first noticed this when she was three and started finger painting. I coached her to draw what she sees and to stay away from the typical stick figures and box houses that most children do. She can now do oils on canvas, and some of her still lifes are "picture perfect." There is no question that Shelly is a highly creative child.

However, creativity is probably something more. It is the ability to perceive, think, create something that did not previously exist. Whereas intelligence is measured by one's ability to understand, repeat, and memorize information, creativity is the process of imagination, innovation, inventiveness, originality; the ability to see relationships between objects. One teacher describes a creative child:

I teach third grade. For two years I heard about this one child, Richard. His previous teachers continually talked about him. You could never tell if they were outraged or amused by this kid's shenanigans. Well, he is in my class now, and believe me, he has lived up to his reputation.

It is not just that he constantly disrupts the class or that he is the class clown. I've had plenty of those. It's that he thinks differently. First, he is always involved in doing what he calls scientific experiments: with plants, animals, and even a few experiments on the other kids. He will answer questions in unusual ways; like when I asked the class what happens after the stomach digests food, he answered, "The blood throws it all over your body." When I asked the class to write a poem, the other kids wrote about the normal things—springtime, flowers, friends, school, family, etc., while he wrote about the pencil sharpener and how lonely it was, grinding away day after day. And it was a great poem!

The school psychologist tested him, at my request. It turned out he did have a rather high IQ, but where he really excelled was on creativity tests. Of course, the psychologist informed me about the limitations of these tests. If we don't even really know what creativity is, how can we begin to measure it? But the test he did take put him in the top 1 percent of all people who had ever taken the test. This really helped me understand and tolerate Richard, and I started providing him with extra, interesting things to keep him occupied.

These major forms of giftedness—mental, motivational, physical, social, and creative—are frequently interrelated. One form of giftedness is likely to cause and/or affect other forms. For instance, the mentally gifted child might also be a highly motivated child, athletically talented and socially skilled. A child might have one form of giftedness or he or she might have all five forms of giftedness.

However, the three types of giftedness of concern to both parents and society are the mentally gifted child, the motivationally gifted child, and the creatively gifted child.

There are two reasons that the other forms of giftedness are not usually considered as important. First, a child is much less likely to have the direction of his life changed by physical or social gifts. Very few people are ever able to make their living directly from physical or social talents. Those few people who do are most certainly highly motivated and, therefore, fall into the other category. Secondly, socially or physically skilled children will not need special attention and understanding, nor will they pose special problems for parents. (In fact, the socially gifted child is perhaps the easiest type of child to raise.) In other words, these children will be raised in the same way one would raise an average child.

The types of giftedness that pose the greatest challenge for parents are the mentally, motivationally, or creatively gifted children. First of all, in order for their gifts to be nurtured and their potential realized, parents will need to provide special attention and understanding. In addition, these children are also likely to present special problems.

The mentally, motivationally, and creatively gifted children are particularly important to future growth and well-being of society. It is the mentally, motivationally, or creatively gifted children who eventually partake in the great orchestration of society; they become our engineers, doctors, scientists, policy-makers, our leaders. It is our gifted children who will have the unique opportunity to shape society; to allocate resources, to find more beneficial ways of doing things; to provide answers to our questions and solutions to our problems. Most important, it is the gifted child who can bring hope to our future.

HOW PARENTS CAN ASSESS GIFTEDNESS

Parents can easily assess if their child is motivationally gifted. All this assessment requires is observation. Does the child focus most of his/her attention on one thing or in one area? Does the child spend large amounts of time and energy on this area of interest? Would the child rather be engaged with this interest than with anything else or to the exclusion of everything else? These are the kinds of simple questions that determine if the child is motivationally gifted.

Assessing mental giftedness is a more complicated task, especially if the child is under the age of six. Intelligence tests administered after the child has reached six years of age are fairly accurate. (We suggest the WISC—Wechsler Intelligence Test for Children—over the Stanford-Binet test.) Parents can inquire about this test at their local schools. If the appropriate school staff is unable (or unwilling) to administer the test to your child, they will be able to direct you to someone who can. It is important to note that intelligence cannot be measured by any group test. Any assessment of intelligence must be administered individually by a psychologist.

Intelligence test scores are far from being the "gospel" measurements of intelligence. At best, these tests provide a reasonable assessment of a child's intelligence. Research indicates that intelligence tests have an unfair bias toward Caucasian, middle-class people. Researchers have isolated as many as sixty variables that contribute to intelligence and creativity—variables that an intelligence test does not measure. However, in most cases intelligence tests will provide parents and schools with a fairly good estimate of children's intelligence, but, unfortunately, not of their creativity.

Parents need to provide the child with some preparation for an intelligence test. A good night's rest and a nutritious breakfast are essential. Two factors that will tend to affect a child's performance are anxiety about the test and rapport with the tester. Surprisingly, a moderate amount of anxiety is beneficial, while too little or too much anxiety is detrimental. A positive rapport between child and tester is also beneficial.

Children who are not prepared are likely to score below their potential. Many parents attempt to reduce a child's test anxiety by telling them the test is not important. One mother discloses this mistake, which she made:

Thomas was seven and going to take an intelligence test. I told him it was just another test and not really important. I said this so he wouldn't be nervous. But actually it was important; it was to see if he qualified for the special mentally gifted minors program in our school district. Not only would he get a better education, but his two best friends were in the program as well.

He went in and was tested. He scored about 125 and he

needed a score of 130. The psychologist called me in after the test and told me he was sure Tom could have done better. Afterward, Tom found out that the test was for MGM. Well, was he disappointed. He said, "Aw, Mom, I didn't know, I could have done a lot better. I just thought they were dumb questions that didn't matter." A year later he was tested again, and he scored 143.

THE PRESCHOOL CHILD

Some parents will want to assess their child's intelligence before the age of six. However, intelligence tests for preschool children are not reliable. The unreliability of these tests is due to both the large developmental variance among preschool children and the young child's inability to fully manipulate symbols (language and numbers). However, there are some simple tests and observations that might shed some light on the intelligence of your child. These tests and observations can only provide a rough idea of average intelligence (or above-average intelligence) in children, and the results are subject to change as the child grows older.

First, the average child will take the first steps toward language usage at the ripe old age of eighteen months. At this age the eighteen-month-old child will have a vocabulary of about ten or twenty words: Mommy, Daddy, doggy, and so forth. These words are used in one-word statements. However, in just a few months, usually by the age of two, words start pouring through the tiny tot's mouth. (Undoubtedly, one of the words the child will use is the all-powerful "No.") In fact, this is called the word-explosion period. About this time the average child also begins combining words.

By the age of two and a half, the average child begins using some plural forms, such as "tall trees." The child also begins using the past tense to some extent and can proudly give a first name. Generally, by the age of three, girls can identify both their age and sex. Most boys will take until they are four to accomplish this feat, for boys develop verbal skills at a slower pace. The above-average child might accomplish these skills somewhat earlier.

One test a parent might want to give a child between the ages of three and six is called the digit repetition test. The instructions are simple. The parent needs to create a list of three sets of three numbers; the first set contains three digits, the second set contains four digits, while the third set contains five digits. For instance:

631	3251	76528
728	2894	52971
346	5036	34759

The parent verbalizes a set of numbers and the child is asked to repeat the number back. Start with the three-digit numbers. If the child doesn't respond, you can say, "I said six, three, one; now you say, six, three, one." Some children will not be able to respond yet. The average child will successfully repeat:

Age:
3   One of the three-digit numbers in any series
3½   Two of the three-digit numbers in any series
4   All of the three-digit numbers in any series
4½   Two of the four-digit numbers in any series
5½   Three of the four-digit numbers in any series
6   One of the five-digit numbers in any series

Another such test requires a block and a chair that the child has previously sat in. Ask the child to put the block in front of the chair, behind the chair, along one side of the chair, along the other side of the chair, and on the chair. As with the previous exercise, some children will not be able to respond yet. The average child will be able to follow:

Age:

3   One command
3½ Two commands
4   Three commands
4½ Four commands
5   Five commands

Another test is called the "What You Must Do" test. Ask the child the following questions:

1. What must you do when you are hungry?
   Acceptable answers are anything that is a food response: "eat," "drink," "cook," etc. Not acceptable are responses such as "tell mommy," "cry," etc.
2. What must you do when you are cold?
   Acceptable answers will involve the process of becoming warm: "put on jacket," "come inside," etc.
3. What must you do when you are sleepy?
   Acceptable answers are any that involve resting: "go to bed," "nap," etc.
4. What must you do if you lose something?
   Acceptable answers are any that have to do with the process of finding or with getting a new one.
5. What must you do before you cross the street?
   Acceptable answers are any that involve caution. Not acceptable is "hurry." The average child will give acceptable answers to:

Age:

3   One question
3½ Two questions
4   Three or four questions
5   All questions

These tests will shed some light on the ingelligence of a child in relation to average scores and development. Once again, parents need to remember that decisions such as school placement should never be made because of a child's performance on any of these tests. However, if your child does do significantly well, you will want a standard intelligence test administered when the child reaches the age of six.

Obviously, some parents will find that they are raising a gifted child. Your child will then need special attention, understanding, and guidance through the problems that might arise from giftedness. This book is for all parents who want to provide the gifted child with every opportunity to reach the full extent of his or her potential.

In summary, the ingredients necessary to assess giftedness in a child are:

1. The ability to recognize that all children are special, unique individuals, each having different talents and aptitudes, successes and achievements.
2. The understanding necessary to distinguish between mental, motivational, physical, social, and creative giftedness; and the understanding of why mental, motivational, and creative giftedness are more important in terms of raising a child.
3. Having an intelligence test administered to a properly prepared child over the age of six.
4. An understanding of the limitations of all tests before the child reaches the age of six.
5. The desire to help your child reach his/her full potential.

Chapter 1
The Gifted Child's Education

THE EDUCATION OF GIFTED CHILDREN IS OF THE GREATEST importance in their lives. Unlike other parents, parents of gifted children cannot take their child's education for granted. Gifted children have special educational needs. Simply put, they need more of it. If each educational subject was a column, the gifted child would need both a taller and wider column than the average child. The problem is that a child with an IQ of 140 will take approximately half the average time to learn any one subject.

The gifted child's special educational needs are often ignored in a regular classroom. When this occurs, boredom is the likely result. Boredom is fertile soil for the development of behavior problems. The following story illustrates this point:

Kevin is a student in the school in which I'm the principal, and he is probably one of the most gifted kids I've ever encountered. The horrible thing is we didn't catch it until the end of second grade.

The first time he was referred to me was the result of a fight he'd been in with his teacher. He refused to play with regular kindergarten toys because they were "dumb." He also refused to play many of the games the teacher had organized, preferring his own solitary play. This was the beginning. His behavior was always bad; he was constantly disrupting the class, and he was not liked by either his teachers or his classmates. And he was not a good student; at the end of the second grade he could barely read or write.

One day I was walking through his classroom. I noticed that while the teacher was explaining something about Navaho Indians, Kevin was busy scribbling numbers. Much to my surprise, he was doing math problems. Not just any math problems, but adult-reasoning problems! The school psychologist gave him an IQ test and he scored 181! He later explained that he never learned to read because "the stories were so dumb." Well, we got a tutor for Kevin, who taught him with science books, and in six months he was reading on a seventh-grade level. His writing, however, never seemed to improve. It was as if he had so much to say, each thought was so important, that to hell with neatness. With his special assignments, he is doing much better.

In the regular classroom, the gifted child must often choose between feigned interest in a boring situation and flaunting authority by showing boredom. Many gifted children have both a high standard of morality and a genuine desire to please adults and, therefore, choose to hide their boredom. The following stories illustrate how children go to extraordinary lengths to do this:

I was walking up and down the aisles of my first-grade class while my students were completing a reading assignment. Suddenly my attention was drawn to this one little boy, Steve. He was turning the pages backwards. I went up to him and asked him what he was doing. He looked down and then smiled and told me, "I always finish the stories so fast, so a while ago I taught myself to read backwards too." He read out loud to me and, indeed, it was backwards. I had him tested and sure enough, he was very gifted.

I'm a school superintendent and recently I was visiting this first-grade class in my district. The classroom was very quiet and everyone was engaged in math problems. I noticed this one child, Marian, was doing something different. She was writing out the numbers 101, 102, 103, etc. I asked her what she was doing and she said, "Oh, Ms. Lewis always makes me write out numbers in the hundreds cause I finish my work so fast. She says I need to be occupied. But you know what?" she asked brightly. "I can already do this up to one million. My brother teaches me to do a lot of things with big numbers."

I had this one very bright girl in my third-grade class. Soon after school began it became apparent that she was far ahead of both the work and her classmates. I began assigning additional reading. I gave her a list of seven books. That night I called her mother to inform her of my plan. Her mother said, "Oh, Lisa is finishing up the last of the seven books. Yes, she read them all in one day so she could have time before bed to finish the book she was reading before she got your reading list. I know it's remarkable. We have trouble keeping enough books in the house for her." What am I supposed to do for a kid like that?

Other gifted students are so disappointed with their regular schoolwork that they learn to ignore their intelligence or giftedness. One such child was recently discovered by a school psychologist:

I'm a school psychologist and once a year I test kids the teachers recommend for our special gifted program. One youngster, Bob, was so referred and on the Stanford-Binet scored 135. I decided that although he was very bright, he should probably stay in the regular classroom. I told him as much and while he seemed disappointed, I felt I had made the right decision.

About three months later I was in his class for another reason and I stopped at Bob's desk to say hello. He was a very nice kid and after a casual conversation he said, "Ya know, I was real upset that I couldn't go into special placement but after a while I knew you were right. In this class, I'm one of the smartest kids and there I would just be average. But you know what?" he said, pointing to another student. "You guys really missed the boat on Norman over there. He is really smart. He is too smart for this class."

Having read somewhere that gifted children recognize other gifted children, I arranged to have Norman tested. This was despite the fact of his average, or sometimes below average, performance. Sure enough, Norman had an IQ of 168. When I asked him to explain his poor performance he said, "If they knew how smart I am, they would just give me more of the same dumb problems. I can't even stand the ones I get now." Apparently he is so smart he just couldn't handle doing regular classwork. He was afraid that he'd just get more of this "regular" work if his teachers were aware of his intelligence.

In general, a gifted child's special educational needs cannot be adequately met in a regular classroom. It seems that the more gifted the child, the more likely this will be true. For instance, children with an IQ of 135–140 might do very well in a regular classroom. They would probably be among the teacher's brightest, most favored students, and be leaders among their classmates as well. As a result, these children are likely to develop a favorable self-image. However, this does not mean that these children wouldn't also benefit from a special program.

The same is not true for the more gifted child. The extremely gifted child needs advanced studies presented at a quick pace. They will be painfully bored in a regular classroom. These children will either choose to suffer through their boredom or create their own stimulation, often at the expense of the rest of the class. In either situation, everyone loses.

What can a parent do?

First, each parent must investigate the local school system. Each school is different, as is each state school system. Certain schools do meet the needs of gifted children, others partially meet these needs, while still others don't even attempt to provide the special educational needs of gifted children. In the past we have paid considerable attention to other important groups of children, with special learning needs, such as physically and emotionally handicapped children, learning-disabled children, and so forth, while totally ignoring gifted children. In recent years, the long-ignored needs of gifted children have been called to the attention of public officials. There has been a call to conduct more research on gifted children, survey existing special programs for them, and allocate more resources toward their education. However, with the current cry for fiscal conservatism and state-controlled school systems, it is unlikely that much, if anything, will change.

Consequently, schools vary considerably in their educational programs for the gifted. Even those states that do have special programs vary in both the type of program and the criteria for entering the program. For instance, California's program for mentally gifted minors (MGM) has a specific requirement for participation in the program—"A minor enrolled in public schools who demonstrates such general intellectual capacity as to place him in the top two percent of all students having achieved his school grade through the state" (CA 1961). This usually means that children can enter MGM with an IQ slightly above 130. Other states leave the decision of who should participate and who should not up to the teachers and school officials. In other words, parents will need to assess their schools in order to determine if there is a program for gifted students and if that program will meet the needs of their child.

It is well beyond the scope of this book to judge individual states and local programs. Instead, we will discuss various ways most public and private schools attempt to meet the needs of gifted children and the pros and cons of each method. Appropriately, our next section is entitled:

THE GOOD AND THE BAD OF GIFTED PROGRAMS

Teachers and administrators have traditionally used one of four different methods, or some combination of the four methods, for educating the gifted. These methods are enrichment, special classes, grouping, and acceleration. Each method has its own advantages and disadvantages. The success of any one program primarily depends on the needs of each child.

Enrichment

Ideally, every child should receive an enriched educational program. It is everyone's hope that all children be provided with the necessary attention and material to reach their full potential. So just what does it mean for a gifted child to be in an enriched program?

An enriched program for gifted children usually means the child is in a regular classroom, doing the regular classwork, plus additional work provided by the teacher. For instance, the gifted child would complete the three regularly assigned math book problems, plus complete an additional two pages from a supplementary, more advanced math book. Or the child would read the standard third-grade reader plus three other books written on a more advanced level.

An enriched program has many benefits for gifted children. First, the child remains in a regular classroom and so interacts with regular classmates. Regular classrooms are likely to mirror real-life situations more than will a group of exclusively gifted children. As mentioned previously, a gifted child can develop a more positive self-image when he or she is at the top of the class and is a leader among peers. Furthermore, when an enrichment program is working, the child receives the benefits of the entire regular program, plus enough additional material to keep boredom at bay and stimulation at a maximum. One exceptional teacher explains how she works out the enrichment program for her third-grade class:

Every year I receive one or two exceptional children in my regular third-grade class. I enjoy these students a great deal. It works out great. They maintain the regular classwork plus the extra material I give them. Each day we meet and discuss their extra assignments and their progress. I truly enjoy watching these gifted youngsters learn, their speed and abilities grow. I don't find any problem providing them with extra work or monitoring their progress. Yes, it is extra work for me, but if I didn't love my work I wouldn't be doing it.

Unfortunately, few enrichment programs are actually able to provide enough enrichment. Many teachers are so overwhelmed just maintaining the regular class that they have neither the time nor the energy to provide individual attention to students. It is very difficult, and often impossible, to see to the needs of thirty to forty students. Therefore, it is not surprising that studies show teachers spend less time with gifted students than with others. One teacher discusses this point in the following monologue:

I have thirty-five students for six hours a day, five days a week, for thirty short weeks, to teach them this incredible bulk of material.

Not only do I have to see to the needs of the slower learners, kids with behavior problems (I have tons of those), the regular average students, and now the gifted students? Look, we decided in this country to educate the masses; that every person deserves the benefits of an education. Does this mean that you will succeed in providing the best education for every single child? No, of course not. Somebody is going to have to take the short end of the stick. Unfortunately, gifted students are prime targets. They are usually the best behaved, easiest-to-handle students, who do all their work and do it well. It's easy to pretend that they are successful members of the class and the educational system as a whole. Asking most teachers to provide additional material and supervision for this perfect kid is just too much. We don't have the time.

Another problem is that it is often not enough for the teacher to provide additional material and supervision. One teacher's experience illustrates this point:

I try to give supplementary materials to those kids who are above the crowd. I know there are those occasional students who know the material and can probably do it as well as I can. But I'm not an expert on gifted children, and I'm never sure how far off I am from meeting their individual needs.

My experience is that I am off more frequently than I'm on. Just this year I had one student who I knew from test results to be gifted. I assigned additional reading and math work. Every week he completed the work and brought it in. I assumed everything was fine. Then one day he approached me and said, "I really don't like the extra work you give me, it seems even easier than our regular stuff." When he showed me what books he was reading and the math he was working on, I saw his point. Here I was, giving him sixth-grade material (he is a fourth grader), but he can do eleventh- and twelfth-grade math!

It seems that for some children, enrichment in a regular class can be an excellent method of meeting their special educational needs. This is especially so if the child's intelligence is not too far from the norm and if individual teachers are both able and willing. However, for other gifted children an enrichment program will not be enough to ensure the fulfillment of educational needs.

Grouping Gifted Students Together

A few schools, and all private schools exclusively for gifted students, segregate the gifted into one class. Grouping can be the best means of providing the gifted child's education. The teacher is able to cover great amounts of material with considerable ease and speed. The gifted child will find stimulation through the teacher and the other students. Some groupings of gifted children are designed so well that each student is able to work independently at his/her own speed and level, thereby receiving the maximum amount of intellectual stimulation. At the very least, grouping eliminates the ever-present problem of boredom in the classroom for most, if not all, students.

Perhaps the greatest benefit of grouping is that the gifted children will have to actually work at their studies. They will no longer stay at the top of the class because of ability alone. A common experience among gifted students grouped together is the discovery (often much to their amazement) that there are other people equally smart and competent. This is an important lesson, especially for the later years, if the children go on to competitive universities and professions.

However, if there is any problem with grouping gifted children together for their education, it is the competition. In some groups, the competition reaches dangerous proportions and a type of "pressure cooker" atmosphere develops. It is often hard to determine which is the greater evil, no competition or too much.

One private school teacher's experience illustrates how the pressure cooker atmosphere often comes not from the students or the teachers, but from the parents:

I taught in a private school for gifted children. It's hard to imagine how very different these kids are. I would always try to remind myself that they were physically and socially just kids, regular kids. That might sound funny, but if you could just see how their parents treat them. It was as though their parents' egos were wrapped up in the children's performance. They treated them like adults, little computers. The questions were always like, "Why isn't Teresa at the top of the class?" "I know Sam can do this kind of work." "He is really on a much higher level, if you would just push him." "Is my kid the brightest of the bright?" I'd even have parents devise formulas based on their child's IQ score that would dictate how well the child should be doing. It was crazy.

The parents and some teachers would put these children under so much pressure. And one thing I noticed about gifted children is that they really want to please. They would kill each other and themselves just to perform. There is just something wrong with the system when these same kids finally enter college and the competition is so stiff that they blow up each other's chemistry experiments, cheat, and sabotage each other's papers. It happens, too, at our finest universities.

On the positive side, the gifted child in a group of other gifted students is likely to thrive socially. They will not feel as different from other gifted children. Furthermore, research has shown that gifted children find relationships with other gifted children richer, more fulfilling and rewarding. Gifted children will find that they have more in common with other gifted children and that they share similar interests. The social aspect of grouping is very important.

All in all, grouping can be the best way of meeting the special educational needs of gifted children. Obviously, not many school districts are able to do this, and private schools are usually out of most families' reach. Fortunately, the next best alternative to grouping is one that many schools are able to provide—that is, special classes.

Special Classes

Some schools offer special classes for gifted children. On the primary level, this means that for one or two hours a day, the gifted child is grouped with other gifted children for enriched reading and math, perhaps even science. On the high school level, the gifted are likewise grouped for some, if not all, of their core subjects. These classes will provide more information and work than an average class, and will proceed at a quicker, more stimulating pace.

A special class program is an excellent way of meeting the special educational needs of gifted children. In this situation, they receive the benefits of both being grouped with other gifted students and remaining in their regular classroom. Also, special classes are sometimes taught by teachers who have been trained in teaching gifted students. One student, Tim, in a special class program, has this to say about it:

I'm in the sixth grade and I go to a really neat school. Before, I went to a regular school and, boy, was it boring. In my new school, though, for my morning classes I go in a different room for enriched reading and math. These classes go so fast that I have to work at keeping up with them. And it's fun. In regular school, well, it's just too easy. I'm way ahead of the class most of the time. I don't mean to brag, but it's true. In the enriched class, though, everyone's smart, that's why we're there, and so it's like a challenge to keep up.

Unfortunately, not many schools offer special classes for their gifted students. Many other schools do so on such a limited basis that they are not really beneficial. For instance, some schools will separate the entire class into three separate groups based on the ability of individual students in reading and math. Often the psychological damage done by this "intelligence stratification" far outweighs the benefits. For other children, especially the extremely gifted, special classes will not be enough to provide adequate educational enrichment.

Acceleration

Many schools use acceleration (the skipping of grades) to meet the needs of the gifted child. Since the public school is geared to the average child, it prescribes six years to cover the material required to enter junior high. The problem is that a child of an IQ of 140 probably could cover the same material in about half the time. As a result, schools will sometimes skip a gifted child one, two, and sometimes as many as three or four grades.

There has been considerable research on children who have been accelerated. Surprisingly, the vast majority of research concludes that gifted children have much to gain from acceleration with little, if any, adverse consequences to bear. Most gifted children are able to skip over one or two grades with relative ease.

Some educators have been concerned that accelerating gifted children means that the child will miss great bulks of material. These educators argue that since the school program progresses sequentially, the child who skips two grades will undoubtedly miss being exposed to important material. They believe that these important gaps in information are covered by the child's intelligence, but that nonetheless, the holes still exist.

However, many teachers of gifted children disagree. One such teacher explains:

I've heard that complaint before: that if you skip a child he will be missing huge blocks of information. I don't buy it. I've had many children enter my class and be three, four, and five levels behind the class. Each level represents approximately one grade. And I have witnessed gifted children rise to class level, go through all the previous material, within two or three months. I don't think those people give the gifted child's intelligence enough credit.

Of course, the question of whether or not a gifted child will be intellectually harmed by acceleration depends on the extent of the child's giftedness. This cost must also be weighed against the benefits to each child for finally being able to operate on his/her educational level. It does seem that for most gifted children the benefits of acceleration far outweigh this cost.

Parents and teachers are also concerned about the social cost of acceleration. The gifted child might be intellectually equal with older children, but are they socially equal? Aren't the gifted children going to suffer because they are developmentally and emotionally behind their classmates?

These are complicated questions, and the answers depend on both the individual children and how many grades they are skipping. In general, a bright child can skip at least one grade with no dire consequences. Each group of any age children holds considerable developmental variance. There will be children a year older but developmentally, socially, and emotionally a year or two behind. Most gifted children enjoy older children and are sometimes able to relate to older children easier than to peers of the same age. For instance, a ten-year-old with an IQ of 140 is likely to enjoy the company of twelve- through fourteen-year-olds simply because they will be on the same intellectual level.

The success of an acceleration of two or more grades depends on the social and physical maturity of the child. Most gifted children are intellectually able to interact with older children but lag far behind in the social-developmental sense. The child's above-average intelligence, coupled with social immaturity, can place the child in a social-outcast position. Ultimately, this can scar a child for life. One mother relates how she handled the problem:

First Shelly skipped second grade. This went well. She excelled in the class and developed close friendships. Then she skipped fourth grade, and this was a mistake. She just couldn't relate to the much older kids. They harassed her and often treated her as some kind of freak. She withdrew and began dreading school and performing poorly. She started having nightmares, very disturbing nightmares.

It got so bad that we soon knew we had to do something. She couldn't be put back, for she was really way ahead of the material. Even though we couldn't really afford to do so, we took out a loan to pay for a private education. Her new school was especially for gifted students. She was so happy after just the first day. She was relieved to find out that she was not a "freak," but one of many. She finds the school challenging and she has made very close friends. It was definitely worth the cost.

One teacher describes a similar experience with an accelerated child:

Frank was very bright and at the top of the class even though he was a whole three years younger. He was such a sweet, quiet child, too. And I think that was the problem; he was naturally very shy and, I guess, socially awkward. Being with older kids didn't help the matter at all. He always preferred the solitary comfort of his individual studies. And it's not that the other kids were necessarily cruel. It's just that they knew he was different and gifted. They didn't ever try to include him in friendships or sports activities. I don't know what's going to happen to this sweet kid. I hope he someday is able to be a happy member of a group, feel liked, and have a sense of belonging.

Surprisingly, the success of acceleration also depends on the physical appearance and ability of a child, who may be accepted or rejected on the basis of his/her sports ability and physical appearance. If the child is athletically inclined and looks older than his age, he will be accepted by the group. It is interesting to know that gifted children are on the average taller, stronger, and healthier than other children.

Another factor parents will want to consider, which affects the success of acceleration, is the child's self-confidence. The self-confident child will interact better with older children, and will be better able to defend and assert himself/herself. So, in assessing whether or not to accelerate a child, parents will want to ask, Is my child shy or outgoing? Is my child confident in social situations? Does he initiate interactions with others; does she ever take a leadership role with others? The self-confident child will find a way through most situations, adapting and eventually making them work for him/her.

In summary, parents considering acceleration for their gifted child will have to consider the following questions:

1. Is my child mentally mature for his age?
2. Does my child like interacting with older kids?
3. Does my child look older than her age?
4. Does my child excel in sports?
5. Is my child self-confident?
6. Does my child want to skip a grade?

The answers to these questions will provide a good predictor of a child's ability to profit from acceleration.

HIGH SCHOOLS

Most high schools (along with most secondary schools) provide adequate education for gifted students; the larger the high school, the more likely it is to have special enriched-education programs for the gifted student. Almost all high schools separate the college-bound students from the rest of the student population. These students (the gifted are almost always included) are placed in college preparatory classes for math, science, English, foreign languages, and sometimes history and social science. The college prep classes provide advanced studies at accelerated rates and are usually composed of dedicated, interested, and able students.

Some high schools are large enough to separate the gifted students for all of their classes. The across-the-board grouping of gifted high school students has many advantages. Schedules are made easier and, therefore, often free the teacher or teachers who have experience or expertise in the instruction of gifted children. These groupings also foster familiarity between teacher and students and friendships among students. Most advantageous of all are the creative curriculum programs these groups can offer by combining and interrelating subjects. One teacher of such a program describes how it works:

I teach for a large Los Angeles school district. Fortunately, we have the resources to separate the gifted students and place them in a program in which they take all their classes together. This class has been taught by me and one other teacher; we both have special training in teaching gifted students. It is amazing how well this system works; I know each and every one of the students and most of their families, and I know their individual strengths and weaknesses. We have been combining studies in an exciting and stimulating way—for instance, European history with European literature, philosophy of the time, and art, relating how literature, philosophy, and art reflect on the history, etc. We are able to give independent assignments to students, too, based on what they're interested in. I know first hand (I have previously taught in private schools) that the education we are providing the gifted students is as good, if not better, than most private schools.

In addition to college prep grouping, most high schools have advanced-placement programs. These are programs in which the academically talented student is able to take college courses while still attending high school. These classes are usually confined to advanced subjects that the high school is unable to provide: English, mathematics, American history, biology, chemistry, physics, and foreign languages: French, German, Spanish, Latin, and Russian, for example. Subjects will vary depending on the individual student needs and the high school they attend. The student travels back and forth between college and high school, receiving credit in both schools.

Through advanced-placement programs, the student is provided a deeper and broader educational experience while still in high school. The student learns the necessary skills for success in college: budgeting of time, organization of large quantities of material, library and laboratory utilization, independence, study with a minimum of supervision, and overall self-discipline. These are undoubtedly important lessons and a definite challenge to the young high school student.

Attending college early through an advanced-placement program is almost always a positive experience. The vast majority of gifted students are genuinely ready to meet the challenge of college work at an early age. One young woman relates her experience:

I really like high school, but realistically I was not getting the education I needed. Socially I was fine, but academically I was bored. In my junior year I was put in advanced placement so I could take math, science, chemistry, and physics courses at college. In retrospect, I realize I never really worked at anything before that point. It was so exciting to be on your own and to really struggle with work. I might not have made it had I not been so motivated. Thanks to that program, I was able to complete my undergraduate studies by the time I was just turning twenty. I took a year off to travel and entered medical school the year after. I think all able students should be allowed to pursue college studies early.

Parents can inquire in their school district as to the specifics of their AP program. Some schools offer a class in advanced placement where the students and a teacher discuss specific problems and provide help and supervision. Other schools have the college professors come to the high school, and still other schools leave the program up to the individual students and colleges. There are a few schools that allow seniors to take all their classes at college. Any way it comes, advanced placement is a good idea.

INTEREST BINGES

A large part of gifted children's education will occur in the home and will come from their parents. The gifted child will be interested in many different things. Their natural curiosity leads them to inquire about every aspect of life. Gifted children need to know the hows and whys about the most unlikely things, things that we often take totally for granted: Who named the potato? Why do garbage men come on Tuesdays? How does sound travel through a wire into the phone? and even insightful psychological inquiries: Why do you get mad after you talk to Ms. Gibson? Why doesn't Daddy like Grandma? Parents often become frustrated at the gifted child's seemingly endless stream of questions.

The following dialogue between a parent and her six-year-old gifted daughter reflects this frustration:

Mother: Are you hungry,, Jeanine? (Mother is fixing lunch.)
Jeanine: Yes. My stomach is making lion growls.
Mother: Well, we'll fill your tummy right up.
Jeanine: Why does my stomach make sounds when I'm hungry?

Mother: It's to tell you that it wants food.

Jeanine: How do those sounds come up?

Mother: Your stomach secretes liquids that gurgle loud enough to hear.

Jeanine: Where does the food go?

Mother: Well, your blood comes to your stomach and picks up the food and carries it to the rest of your body.

Jeanine: Does it carry it everywhere in my body?

Mother: Yes.

Jeanine: Even my little finger?

Mother: Yes, even your little finger.

Jeanine: How can a sandwich fit in my little finger?

Mother: Oh, well, your stomach breaks the food into tiny little bits before the blood comes to get it.

Jeanine: How does my tummy do that?

Mother: Jeanine, maybe you'd like to play on the swing before lunch.

This incredible thirst to know will project the gifted child through interest binges. The child picks a subject and becomes totally immersed in it. A sister of one such gifted child describes this phenomenon:

My mother has always said that Jimmy was different from day one, and I believe it. I can trace our childhood with the different obsessions he had. The first one I remember was dinosaurs. He read everything about dinosaurs; he built model skeletons of dinosaurs, he drew pictures of dinosaurs, and he talked dinosaurs. Everything you ever wanted to know about dinosaurs and more—much, much more. Then came science. He read all twelve volumes of the Encyclopedia of Science by the time he was eight! Then he narrowed in on astronomy; my parents bought a telescope. Next came chemistry, then geology—he started rock collecting, coin collecting, archery, baseball, stamp collecting. Then golf. He played golf every day during high school. Then the stock market and finances, communism, and finally, economics as a whole. He is now getting his Ph.D. in economics and math. And his career looks very promising. Obviously, he is a very focused individual.

Parents of gifted children will want to support their interest binges. Try to do anything and everything possible to help the child's exploration of any area of interest; help find the books and the material. Be willing to discuss the subject past the point of boredom; whenever possible, coordinate outings with interests, such as a visit to the museum, planetarium, aquarium, zoo, historical sights, etc.; and when possible, purchase that chemistry set, telescope, or coin-collecting magazine. Parents who do support the child's interest binges will not only be encouraging the child's exploration of the world, but will also be doing a great deal to enrich the child's education.

PARENT PROGRAMS FOR ENRICHMENT

Taking parental support of interest binges one step further, parents can start their own enrichment program for gifted students. This can be done individually or in a group. An enrichment program can be an excellent addition to any school program. It requires two valuable things from parents: time and energy. We all know how precious those two things are, but when a parent is able to provide them, fantastic things can happen!

A program for individual students is obviously easier to manage. Parents will want to start by providing supplemental reading material on each subject offered in school: math, science, history, etc. Librarians can often provide parents with the necessary direction to supplemental reading material. In addition, parents will always want to encourage the gifted child's interest on any subject with extra reading material. If the child inquires about marine life, astronomy, the design of cars,

Abraham Lincoln, or elephants, parents can plop down a book on that subject in front of the child the next day. This is the first and most important step to providing enriched education.

Next, parents can increase the number of educational outings, on which they take their children. Trips to museums, aquariums, planetariums, zoos, wildlife parks, and historical sites will all serve to enrich the gifted child's education. Parents can often arrange visits to or through industries, factories, and institutions that might be of interest. Many companies offer their own guided tours, which only take a phone call to arrange. The following stories illustrate how these activities are not only educational but fun for both parent and child:

My son is eight and doing very well in school, even though I'm often disappointed with its programs. I try my best to provide extra education. The other day, Terry started asking about our judicial system. I tried to explain as much as he could understand. He seemed very interested, so I got him some books on the subject. After he read them, he seemed even more interested. So I took a day off work, pulled him out of school, and took him to the superior court for a day. He saw the whole system in action—the judge, the jury, the prosecuting and defense lawyers, and the defendant. He also heard the testimony of witnesses and police officers. Even I was fascinated.

In our area there is a company that makes some of the best chocolates in the country. One day when my children and I were indulging ourselves, the question of how they make chocolate came up. The question was probably spurred by *Willie Wonka and the Chocolate Factory*. Well, I remembered a few years ago my friend had gotten a summer job at this factory and had told me that they offer tours through the company. I called and arranged to be in the next guided tour that was being held, about two months away. It was great and the kids couldn't believe it. They had never seen the inside of a factory. I think it gave them a new perspective on things. It's so easy to take for granted that all the things you need and use magically appear in a store. Now they realize that every single product has many people behind it, making it for us.

I remember as a child how my mother would pack up all the neighborhood kids in our station wagon and take us somewhere. She'd take us to all the museums, the aquarium, the zoo and the planetarium, parks, etc. None of the other mothers ever took anyone anywhere. I don't think most of the kids would have traveled off the block if it weren't for my mother. This went on for about seven years. One by one, each of the neighborhood kids has sought my mother out, after moving away, to tell her how much they learned from her and the outings she took us on.

Initiating an enriched program on a group level is much harder, but ultimately very worthwhile. The best way to do it is by organizing the interested parents of gifted children into running an enriched after-school program for this purpose. Most school districts will provide the names and addresses of other parents. Send a polite letter of introduction and intention to these parents, with a prearranged first meeting time and place. Most schools will also be able to provide after-school classroom space as well.

Depending on the number of interested parents, each parent can volunteer one afternoon a week or month to supervise an after-school activity. Parents can volunteer to supervise activities that they are personally interested in. Children should not be forced to take any "class," but should be interested in the activity also. For some classes, a small fee might be required. Perhaps the entire group can involve itself in fund-raising activities, garage sales, a car wash, cake bakes, etc. This could provide special funds to help the cost.

The following is a partial list of extracurricular classes that parents could provide:

1. Book and poetry discussions
2. Creative writing class
3. Math workshop
4. History—reading and discussion
5. Political awareness or current events
6. Arts and crafts
7. Understanding the art world
8. Playing with puzzles and games
9. Lecture series—this would mean organizing interesting professionals to come in and discuss their fields.
10. Outing day—museums, planetarium, industry, etc.

Obviously, there are endless possibilities. Parents can ask both the children and teachers for suggestions. In the programs that have already been established, parents have been amazed at how many people in the community are willing to help. Not only is volunteering your time to this cause worthwhile, but it is also a fun, enriching activity for you. One woman, who is involved in such a program in California, explains how well it has worked:

We service an area within a fifty-mile radius and have over three hundred adults and eighteen hundred gifted children involved. Our program is very necessary; the schools just don't do enough for these kids. Parents pick subjects that they are particularly interested in and they devise a program. Each month we send a flier to the parents explaining what's offered, where, when, and the fee, if any (fees never go over three to five dollars). Everything is totally voluntary, and we get no assistance from the schools. It is so exciting and I think I'm learning as much as the kids!

In summary, the ingredients necessary to provide your gifted child with special education are:

1. An understanding of the gifted child's need for special education.

2. An understanding of the costs and benefits of the four basic ways that schools usually try to meet these needs: enrichment, grouping, special classes, and acceleration.
3. When possible, attempting to match your child with the program that's best for him/her.
4. Supporting the gifted child's interest binges.
5. Initiating your own group or individual enrichment program.

Chapter 2

The Underachieving Gifted Child

SOME GIFTED CHILDREN ARE UNDERACHIEVERS—THAT IS, they just do not work up to their ability level. The first sign is usually a decline in the gifted child's grades or school reports. Next, the teacher's reports begin piling up; she is not completing assigned tasks, he is not paying attention, she is performing poorly on tests, he is performing far below potential, she is failing in math, and so on. Parents and teachers alike throw their hands up in dismay, "Why, the child is so bright, what could be the problem?"

The search begins, and this search for the problem almost always takes place in the realm of psychology. Psychology has permeated every aspect of our society and has affected the way we view ourselves and our children. We see each person as a tangled web of hidden motivations, desperate needs, and mysterious complexes. This overpsychologizing has adversely affected the way we handle children, especially gifted children, and their behavior problems.

The first thing parents learn from psychology is that if their child is misbehaving, they obviously are responsible. Parents spend many hours wondering what went wrong with their child-rearing practices. Soon they are convinced of their guilt and all too easily take the blame for their child's misbehavior.

Typically, parents offer a handful of explanations for what is wrong with their child. We have heard thousands of such explanations: "I toilet trained her too late," "He does that because he doesn't have a strong father," "He is having an identity crisis," "He is just testing his limits," "Gifted children are just more intense and difficult." Even though these explanations may have some validity, how do they help overcome the underachievement of your gifted child?

The following case demonstrates just how far many parents carry their psychological beliefs:

Gene, age ten and a gifted child, was becoming a terror at school, throwing tantrums at least once a day. He would scream, throw things, jump up and down, and even bang his head against the wall—and of course, he was completing almost none of his work. When his teachers confronted his parents, the parents would assure the school that they would handle the tantrums at home. However, nothing changed, and each day Gene seemed to get worse. After a meeting with the family it became clear that the father was convinced all of these problems were related to the fact that besides being gifted, Gene was a very emotional child. Therefore, when the child went into his daily rages at home, Gene's father would say things like, "Boy, are you upset today," and "You sure have a lot of anger stored up inside that you need to get out." These communications did little except reassure Gene that he had good reason to be acting the way he was, and that it was both healthy and necessary for him to release his pent-up feelings lest the feelings become bottled up inside.

Just as during the McCarthy era we found Communists in every closet, we now find emotionally disturbed, learning-disabled, hyperactive children in every home. Our labels abound: When a child is energetic, he is hyperactive; when a child is troubled, she is emotionally disturbed; when a child has trouble learning, even though she is gifted, she is learning disabled. One perceptive physician sarcastically remarked, "There must be an epidemic of hyperactive children, because all of a sudden thousands of children are being referred to doctors for medication." Actually there is an epidemic of labeling children. Even calling a child "gifted" can serve as a label! This mania is at the very least misleading and at the most, dangerous.

Let's look at the major reason for the popularity of labels. Labels provide a convenient excuse not to have to deal with the inappropriate behavior. In other words, parents are able to abnegate their control of the child. We have heard from many parents such statements as, "Oh, of course he is hard to handle because he is gifted." "Despite his high IQ score, he is hyperactive." "We let Johnny throw tantrums because he needs an emotional outlet."

Gifted children will find a loophole in every system. These children realize, too, that their label gives them a fine excuse to misbehave, one of the more effective loopholes. An eight-year-old client made this point in the following conversation:

Gavin: You don't have to ask my mom why I'm not doing well at school. I can tell you.
Therapist: OK. You tell me.
Gavin: Well, it's because I'm gifted.
Therapist: What's that?
Gavin: You should know; you're the psychologist.
Therapist: I can't remember, why don't you tell me?
Gavin: It means that I need more than other kids, you know, 'cause I'm so smart. And that's why I have trouble—because I'm too good for the school.

Compare the gifted child's underachievement to some petty offense that you have committed, like driving over the speed limit. Why did you do it? Are you emotionally disturbed, hyperactive? Gifted? Did your parents toilet train you too late? Are you still having an identity crisis? Of course not. You drove over the speed limit because you wanted to and thought you could get away with doing so.

The same reasoning usually applies to the underachieving gifted children. If they think they can get away with something, they might try it. Almost all behavior problems are just this simple. After a little thought, you will realize that trying not to do something that you don't want to do is actually healthy, not a sign of mental illness.

In fact, most parents could trace the start of the gifted child's underachievement to the first time the child was actually challenged. Gifted children often go through an early education with incredible ease; every assignment, problem, or learning task is met with little or no effort. These children are used to accomplishing a great deal more than the average child, without ever working. Suddenly, the first problem or assignment comes along that requires work from the gifted child. At this point, having no previous experience with work that requires real effort, the gifted child may simply give up. The following two cases illustrate this point:

For the first three years of school, my only child, Laura, attended a public school. After the middle of her first year the teacher insisted on an IQ test. She was tested and scored somewhere above 170. The school thought it best if Laura skipped two grades. I guess it was all we could do, because my husband and I were just completing our graduate degrees and we had absolutely no money for a private school. And Laura seemed to be doing so well in public school. She could do all the work perfectly.

Finally, my husband and I graduated, and before too long we had enough money for a private school. We found this one school for exceptional students that had an excellent reputation. Laura was excited about her new school for about a week. Then came her complaints: "They're very strict, Mommy," "They don't explain stuff enough," etc. Then came the trouble. She dropped further and further behind. Pretty soon she practically stopped doing her work. I guess it was just too dramatic a switch from being at the top of her class to being just an average student.

Thomas was very bright, always at the top of his class until high school. It seems the high school really separated the kids, and Thomas was put in this special program for the top thirty kids in a large school of 2,500. They were to take all their core subjects together: math, science, English, history, and social science. All of a sudden, Thomas started falling behind, not completing his homework, and performing poorly on tests. The teachers informed us that if he didn't start doing better he would be dropped from the program. We just don't know what to do; we really wanted him to get the special attention and assignments.

All parents become upset when their children are operating below potential, and this seems even more distressing when the child is gifted. Some parents try everything to reach the underachieving gifted child—all to no avail. After countless battles and great expenditures of energy, the frustrated parent gives up and relinquishes control. The following story is typical of the frustration these parents feel:

Warner was nine and extremely gifted, but he was obsessed with only one thing: chess. He couldn't care less about school, math, science, reading, etc. It was all we could do to even get him to go. Oh, sure, we were proud of his ability—he won almost every tournament he entered—but we didn't want his whole life to be centered on one thing, anything. We tried everything, I mean everything. You know, he would sneak chess books into school and boards into his room at night. He was totally failing in school. We even took him to a shrink. Finally, we just gave up trying.

Unfortunately, many parents end up abnegating all control over the obstinate child. This is the first mistake.

Other parents will, at first, attempt to punish the underachieving gifted child. There are good reasons why punishment does not often work and why it is a bad idea. First of all, the child will undoubtedly start associating schoolwork with punishment. All too soon, school will seem more painful to the child. Secondly, parents usually use what's called a punishment contract in order to discipline. A punishment contract occurs when the parent tells the child to do something or else he will receive a punishment. Examples of such statements are, "If you don't start getting better grades we will take away your TV," "If you don't start completing your homework you will be grounded," and so forth. The trouble is that in these cases the parent is giving the child a choice as to whether or not she should do a certain behavior. Very often the child opts for the punishment. Finally, besides being ineffective, punishment can do a great deal to erode the warm feelings between parent and child, while replacing them with considerable animosity.

In addition to punishing gifted children, there are many different kinds of ineffective communications. Some actually encourage misbehavior, others come closer to a demand, but none really spells out what the child "has to" do. Wishy-washy communications work with some children; these are the easy-to-raise children who are not easily frustrated. However, the gifted child needs a communication devoid of ambiguity, one which the child knows the parents mean one hundred percent.

The following are typical types of ineffective communications:

Kevin was a top student and usually not much trouble. However, one day the teacher caught Kevin cheating on an exam. Consumed by her anger, she yelled, "Don't ever let me catch you again." Two weeks later Kevin was caught cheating again.

Kevin probably won't stop cheating. In fact, this type of communication often encourages the misbehavior. Kevin's teacher never told him to stop cheating. Instead, she told Kevin only to never let her catch him. All of us can remember that a dare was something we took as a challenge, an incentive to engage in a behavior. It is certainly not a direct demand to stop the misbehavior.

The gifted child obviously understands your meaning—but that doesn't necessarily help. One of the jobs of a child is to test out her world, including her parents and teachers. Gifted children try to figure out who is credible and who is not, when people are bluffing and when they are serious. In other words, they are looking for loopholes, and this type of ineffective communication provides a perfect loophole. Gifted children can also be master manipulators, more than able to use every loophole to their advantage. Another example:

Joann was a bright student, but she had constant trouble getting her homework done and turned in on time. Both her parents and her teachers would communicate to her to "Try," "Try harder," "Really try and give it your best effort." Still, Joann would persist in turning in her work late.

This kind of communication, telling a child to try, is in reality the same as telling them you don't expect them to accomplish the task. Telling a child to try is appropriate in activities like sports, where ability is in question; for instance, "Try to hit a home run," "Try to finish first in the race," "Try to finish the jigsaw puzzle," are all appropriate statements. However, it is not appropriate to tell gifted children to try to do what they are perfectly capable of.

To further make the point, imagine you are at a hall listening to a lecture. The lecturer turns to his audience and says, "Please *try* to stand up: I know you could all stand if you just tried." It would make sense for the lecturer to say "try" only if he thought that the people in the audience had major obstacles preventing them from standing. The same is true of your communication to your children. Telling them to try to do something is really communicating that you question their ability to accomplish the task. The real message that comes across is, "I don't really expect that you will do this."

Another type of ineffective communication occurs when the parent probes the child for the cause of the underachievement. The following is a dialogue between a parent and an eight-year-old child:

Parent: "Why did you fail the math test?"
Child: "I dunno."
Parent: "Didn't you study for it?"
Child: "Yes."
Parent: "Did you do all your homework?"
Child: "Yes, I think so."
Parent: "Then, why did you fail?"
Child: "I dunno."
Parent: "You know why you failed."
Child: "Why?"
Parent: "Are you getting smart with me?"
Child: "No."
Parent: "Why did this happen then?"
Child: (Desperately) "I guess 'cause I didn't really study."
Parent: "You just said you studied. Now, are you lying to me?"

This is typical of the conversations that can develop when parents ask "Why?" Parents often feel that their children must have a good reason for their underachievement, and they will insist that their children explain the reason to them. However, as children are put under pressure to explain themselves, they inevitably make up stories. When a child gets caught in a lie, the parent gets even angrier.

Asking children to explain themselves does nothing to change their behavior. Children, even very bright children, are just not capable of sophisticated introspection or self-analysis. They rarely know why they do anything beyond a simple "I wanted to." Psychologists have spent many years trying to uncover the secrets of motivation. How could a child possibly tell you more than "I wanted to" or "I dunno," especially if this is the truth!

Parents should seek explanations of behavior from their gifted children only if there is an explanation that could make the behavior acceptable. If no such explanation exists, however, then why ask the question? If your child has just failed the third test in a week or if your child consistently is late with homework, what answer would cause you to say, "Oh, that's a good reason—so continue"? Very often we miss the real point in our psychological search for reasons, which is that the child is to stop the behavior.

A similar type of ineffective communication frequently employed with gifted children can be demonstrated in the following conversation between a father and his eight-year-old son, Eddie.

Eddie, you know you are a very smart, gifted young person. You're capable of doing anything you want. There is no reason for you to be falling behind in school. And that's the point, Eddie—it is up to you to do your best. This country is founded on the principle of individualism; each person is responsible for his or her own success or failure. And the reason our country is great is because individuals are able to strive to work to achieve the most that they can. I know you can do it, Eddie.

Very well put, one must admit. Sadly enough, Eddie, even though he is gifted, understood very little of what his father said to him. When asked to repeat in his own words what his father had told him, Eddie said, "Well, something about the country and doing your best." Eddie's father is guilty of overexplaining in order to motivate, inspire, or otherwise convince the child to do better in school. While this kind of reasoning or inspiration is an important part of parenting, it rarely convinces a determined gifted child.

The real problem with overexplaining is that it is based on the belief that once children understand why they should or should not do something, their behavior will change. This is patently not true. How many millions of people continue to smoke, overeat, and drink when they are aware of the many reasons why they should not. If explaining and reasoning doesn't work even with many adults, how can one expect it to work with children?

When reasoning is not backed up by a parental demand, the child usually has a choice in the matter. The child is allowed to decide from her perspective whether the reason is important enough to influence her behavior.

The child will often adopt the viewpoint that she doesn't have to do something if she can prove there is a flaw in her parents' thinking. And gifted children are particularly adept at finding flaws in everyone's thinking. If you tell a quick-witted child she will have a tough time in life if she doesn't do well in school, she may respond with a list of names of successful people who quit, flunked, or were thrown out of school. The stories of Thomas Edison, Albert Einstein, and Carl Sandburg are frequently employed in this regard.

Reasoning with children often leads to heated discussions or arguments instead of leading to the desired behavior. Through arguing, the gifted child learns that he can postpone things and perhaps even modify his parents' stand. In addition, overexplaining and reasoning usually convey to a child that the parent is not really sure about his or her stand.

Parents will usually overexplain issues in an attempt to inspire their children to do what they want them to do. However, there is really no way to inspire someone to do something; you cannot control another person's emotions. The truth is that many children do not like school, and there is really nothing you can do to change this fact. However, this does not mean you cannot change your child's behavior and therefore enhance his educational experience.

Such was the case of Arnold, a gifted child of twelve, who was doing A-level work in mathematics but was failing every other subject. He had even received special tutoring, to no avail. When his parents came to family therapy, the following dialogue took place:

Therapist: Why is it, do you suppose, that Arnold does so well in one subject, yet seemingly has such difficulty with history, English, and geography?

Father: That's easy. Arnold loves math. He'd rather do his homework in math than watch TV or play outside with the kids. He's a fanatic. Even all of the dice and card games he plays are math oriented. He's just a born mathematician, I guess.

Mother: And as much as he adores working with numbers, that's how much he hates all of his other subjects. That's why he never does his homework in those classes. Heaven knows, we've tried to get him interested in history. We've taken him to plays about famous people from the past, we even took a trip to Washington, D.C. But he just doesn't care about that stuff.

Arnold: It's just too hard remembering all those names and dates. All of those people lived so long ago. Who cares about them anyway?

At first, it would be easy to conclude that Arnold, no matter what, would never be interested in anything but mathematics. The fact is that Arnold's apparent disdain for history and English was mainly a reaction to his parents continually trying to inspire him. Eventually his parents realized how fruitless their attempted manipulation was; they decided to leave Arnold's emotions alone and instead to just demand that he do his homework in all his other subjects as well as he did in math. Several months later Arnold's parents called to say that Arnold was not only getting B's and A's in *all* of his subjects, but that he was now as enthusiastic about history and English as he had previously been about math.

Of course, not all children would have responded the same way in this situation. Some would have gone right on hating those classes while doing their homework and improving their grades. However, in this case, as in many others we have seen, when the parents focused directly on changing the behavior of the child, his emotions were left free to take care of themselves.

If the communications discussed so far are not effective in changing the problem of underachievement, what is left?

After parents have tried to inspire, reason with, threaten, and plead with their child unsuccessfully, the only alternative remaining for them is to clearly and emphatically *demand* that the child change his behavior. Demands differ from all the previously discussed communications in that they are emphatic and precise. A case history will illustrate the use of demands:

Scott, age twelve, was having great difficulties in a school to which he had recently transferred. Whereas he had been an A-minus student at his old school, his grades had fallen to D's and F's, and he was cutting classes as well. Testing showed that he had a rather high IQ. It was therefore felt by the school counselor that Scott had an emotional problem that was causing him to perform badly in school.

When Scott and his parents came to family therapy, his mother mentioned that she wanted Scott to enjoy school and get along with his teachers and classmates. She thought he was just like his father in that when he didn't like something, there was "no way on earth" you could get him to do it. Both parents mentioned that they had tried various methods of getting Scott to stay in class and do his homework and not to cut class.

The therapist then pointed out to Scott's parents: "It seems to you that you have tried everything to get Scott to stay in school and do his homework. However, the one thing I haven't heard you say is that you have *demanded* that Scott do these things." "But what can we say?" questioned Scott's mother. The therapist then asked her to think of a time when Scott did not want to do something but she was able to get him to do it anyway. She thought awhile and at first stated that she never could get him to do anything if he really didn't want to. Finally Scott himself interrupted and said, "What about those dumb family picnics you make me go to?" The therapist then asked Scott's mother to remember exactly what she said to her son about his going to the picnics. She stated, "I just tell him, 'You're going.'" "And then what happens?" asked the therapist. "He usually complains and stalls; finally I just have to tell him, 'Get in the car.'" The therapist then pointed out that she was very successful in getting Scott to do what she wanted when she made a demand and stuck with it. "However," he added, "no one has demanded, the way you do with family picnics, that Scott go to school and do his homework."

Beginning immediately after this session, Scott's parents personally took him to school and insisted that he stay there to do his work. This he did, and within a few weeks he was participating at school and doing his homework, and his teacher reported that his grades were greatly improved.

How do demands differ from all other things parents say to their children? Essentially, there are only two types of demands. One is that the child stop doing something, and the other is that she begin to do something. In the first category are examples such as:

"Don't cut classes."
"Don't hurry through your work."
"Don't use the game until after your study period."

Those demands that indicate the child is to begin to do some action include:

"Do your homework now."
"Turn off the TV now."
"Come straight home after school today."

A clear demand is simply a statement of the rules, such as, "You are not ever to cut school again." It includes a reference to when the child is to do the behavior or for how long he is to cease doing it. "Turn your TV off" is not a clear demand because this statement does not tell the child when to turn the TV off.

There is a significant difference between these demands and the ineffective communications mentioned previously. The difference is that all nondemands leave the choice of whether to do the behavior with the child. When parents ask their child to do something, the child has the choice of whether or not to comply. When reasoning is the approach, the final decision is left with the child. The same is true of warnings, threats, and encouragements. Only demands make it clear that there is no choice for the child about the particular behavior.

It may be difficult at first for the reader to accept the idea that children do what is demanded of them by their parents. All parents, however, can think of particular situations in which their child has been told in no uncertain terms what he is to do or not do. In these cases, the child senses that his parents really mean what they are saying, that there is no choice in the matter, and he does as he has been told. For example, nearly all parents get their children to go to school, to not play in the street, to brush their teeth, to stay off the roof, to take baths, and so on. Many children do not want to do these things and frequently resist and complain about having to do them. The reason they do them is that in these cases parents are quite sure that these things are important and their communications reflect the intensity of their convictions.

Many parents do not believe that a clear demand will work with their child. In our clinical practice we give a money-back guarantee that parents are capable of getting their children to obey a demand. We have never lost. To prove that you are sometimes a successful parent, recall a time when your child misbehaved and you were successful in preventing her from watching TV or in making her go to her room. The messages you used in these situations were no doubt quite different from the nondemands we talked about earlier. On these occasions you did not say, "I dare you not to go to your room," or "Why don't you go to your room," or "I will punish you if you don't go to your room." Instead, you probably stated, "Go to your room now, and stay there!" and the tone in your voice signaled to your child that you really meant this, that you were not fooling around.

This demonstrates that parents are powerful figures when they use clear communication. We are not saying that punishment changes behavior, but rather that when you make a clear demand your child will obey. Parents often make the clearest demands when they decide to punish children. All you have to do is use the same clarity and fervor in stopping problem behavior as you do when you punish your children. Why not produce the anger and commitment in the beginning, instead of after the misbehavior has driven you crazy?

Parents may question, "You mean that to demand my child do better in school is all I need to do?"

There *is* something more. However, it is crucial to learn to state a clear demand in unambiguous terms. In addition to the words, though, it is also necessary that the child know you really mean what you are saying, that you are not *asking* him to do something, that you are not *wishing* he would do it, but rather that you are *telling* him to do it.

Parents differ in the way they speak when they really mean

what they are saying. Some parents raise their voices a little, others get a certain look on their faces, still others stand differently or look directly in the child's eye when they speak. Whatever the case, every child learns that there is something his parents do when they mean that he is to do exactly what they say. Think for a moment about the way parents would react to their child's stepping out into the street as a car was approaching. They would not ask the child to get back on the curb, they would not tell him that if he doesn't get out of the street he might get hurt. What they would do would be to yell to the child in the clearest and most emphatic terms they know that he is to get back on the sidewalk.

It is often quite natural for parents, in the course of making demands of their children, to become emotional to some extent. In spite of what some experts say, it is unreasonable to expect that parents not get angry at their children some of the time. Expressing this anger is also an essential part of a meaningful message. The parent who tries to cover up these feelings usually ends up with a powerless communication, because the parental emotions are cues that help a child realize that what has been said has been meant. Without these cues a child may feel that his parents' message is really not very important.

Of course, you are likely to have more difficulty if your child has been underachieving for any period of time. One clear demand after five years is not likely to be enough to convince your child that you mean what you say. The gifted child might even think to himself, "Oh, no, my parents read another child psychology book and they have found another new approach!" The child is bound to test your new method by continuing or even escalating the problem behavior. At this point you must ask yourself, "What action can I take to back up the demand?" You as the parent must demonstrate that you mean what you say and also that you will follow through to prove it. The action you decide on should be well thought out in advance so the child never detects ambivalence or fluctuation in your demand.

The action will also vary with each problem behavior. For instance, if your child is leaving school without permission, you should first state the demand clearly: "You must never leave the school grounds before school is over." Next, if that proves ineffective, you will need some kind of action to back up the demand, such as driving your child to school and waiting outside the classroom door if necessary in order to get the message across. After doing this for several days you might then ask the school authorities to call you the minute your child does not show up in any of his classes and give them the phone number where you can be reached. One parent, after hearing about this approach, stated: "Why should I go to school? What about my job?"

We are not saying parents should go to school, we are saying that a parent who really means what he is saying *would* go to school to prove the point. In addition, we are not suggesting that you repeat high school with your child, but only saying that if it is really important, a few days of missed work will save you months and years of heartache in the long run.

If the problem is that your child is not doing her homework and hasn't been doing it for quite a while, a clear demand would be: "You are to do your homework every day between two and five o'clock." Then you might restate your demand in no uncertain terms every day, and check during that time to make sure she is complying. These actions will leave no doubt in the child's mind that you are serious about your demands.

Physical reinforcement is not to be confused with physical punishment or hurting the child in any way. An example of physical punishment would be a parent's telling her child to go to bed and then spanking the child when she does not do as told. The parent in this case has sent a clear message: "I did not mean that you have to go to bed. When I meant was that if you don't go to bed you get a spanking." A parent who uses physical reinforcement instead of punishment would take the child to the bedroom and even place the child in bed, if necessary. By doing this a parent is saying, "I really meant it when I said that you have to go to bed."

The child in this case learns that when his parents say something, they back it up. These follow-throughs are not enacted in such a way as to connote to the child, "See, I'm bigger and stronger than you." Rather, the parent simply uses the minimum amount of force necessary to communicate that this is something the child has to do.

You are bound to be surprised at the results of simple, direct communication of demands. Once your child stops the problem behavior, you will be in a much better position and frame of mind to build an even more loving and warm relationship with your child. Everyone will be a winner.

There is only one necessary ingredient left once a parent is committed to changing the gifted child's underachievement in school and knows the power of clear, effective demands. That ingredient is structure, and it must first come from the parent.

The first step is to determine how much structure is appropriate. Contact the school and ask the teacher or teachers how much time is necessary each day for the child to both study the school material and complete the assigned tasks. This figure should vary among children, increasing with age and the difficulty of the school. We suggest that parents add a half hour to an hour to any time figure the school gives. This will be the period of time the child spends at home in a study period.

Too often parents make the mistake of saying, "You are to study right here when you get home and you are not to leave until you have finished." This leaves the child the decision of how much studying is necessary or determining when they are actually finished. Most children will rush through their work or not even complete it in order to be through. Setting aside a specific amount of time that never varies eliminates these problems. If the child does finish before the time is up, the parent can then instruct the child to read, study further, or to work ahead. It is also important not to let the child decide when to have the daily study period. Parents should pick the time and not allow it to vary based on the child's wishes.

Next, pick a place in your home where the child might do the work. This place should not be private, such as the bedroom or den. Private places will leave children to their own devices, and before long they will be doing everything but studying. Instead, the study period should take place in a public area, one where a parent can easily monitor the child's activity.

Third, parents would be wise to inform the child that each and every day, each and every school book is to be brought home. Children often use the excuse of forgetting a book in order to escape a homework assignment.

Fourth, provide the child with a binder (or some other mechanism) that allows for easy organization of school material. Simple organization is often the key to scholastic success.

All parents have to do now is to make the demands to the child. For instance:

"Each day you are to carry home every single school book."
"Every day when you get home from school at two-thirty, you will
    spend the next three hours studying your schoolwork."
"This studying will be done at the kitchen table."
"There will be no exceptions."

The last thing a parent should do is to monitor the gifted child's work. Some parents might want to insist on a daily list of assigned work and then check each item at the end of a day. Other parents might want the daily list to come from the child's teacher. Some parents might even want to rate the child's work each day. In this case, use the scoring of 0—incomplete, 1—poor, 2—fair, and 3—good. The child should be forced to complete all 0's and perhaps redo all 1's. At the end of the week, total the child's points and offer a reward for a good performance!

In general, the best rewards are also the simplest. Praise, a warm hug, or a pat on the shoulder are enough for most children. The older child might benefit from adding the points and putting them toward some pleasurable activity—a ski trip, a picnic, or a trip to the beach. In this way, the parent is rewarding the process of maintaining good study habits rather than rewarding any specific outcome, such as a grade.

However, money is usually not a good reinforcer. The child is likely to learn that money is the only worthwhile motivator. In later years, such as during college, when money is no longer a reinforcement, the person is unable to become motivated to study. In most cases, though, a reward system can often make the most difficult tasks into pleasurable ones.

Once you institute the forced study period on the underachieving gifted child, you are certain to see a dramatic improvement. The child is forced to live up to his potential and, in the process, he might even realize that he enjoys doing so. All a parent really needs is to provide the structure and make the demand.

In summary, the ingredients necessary to make the underachieving gifted child begin operating at his/her full potential are:

1. Understanding that most gifted children who underachieve do so because they want to, they are bored, they don't know how to actually work, and/or their parents let them get away with it.
2. Understanding that it is probably a mistake to allow the child to control the situation, to punish the child, or to communicate ineffectively what the child is to do.
3. Provide the child with necessary structure.
4. Make a clear demand that every day the child is to study, at this place and for this amount of time.
5. Reward the underachieving gifted child for becoming the high achiever he was meant to be.

Chapter 3

Beyond Education:
Creativity and the Gifted Child

IMAGINE—THE GREAT CREATOR AND HIS FAITHFUL SERVANT in the process of creating the many different shapes of men and women:

Creator: By George! I've done it. I gave this batch all my best stuff: superior mental abilities, skyrocketing cognitive acceleration powers, ease and speed of understanding, the skills to analyze and retain large bulks of information. This batch will be my most dazzling performers—the statesmen, leaders, great teachers, and artists of the world. Their actions will direct the great book of life.

Faithful Servant: Ah, wise and fair, great and noble Creator, aren't you forgetting something?

Creator: What could I be forgetting? After all, Faithful Servant, I am omnipotent, omniscient, infinitely wise. Why, some even say I am omnipresent, too.

Faithful Servant: Well, yes, this is true. But will superior mental facilities be enough when they reach the end of the twentieth century? You know, that period where you really throw the book at them?

Creator: (heavy sigh) Yes, that is a tricky time. All the little people begin to suspect that I'm about to pull the plug. Some even stop caring.

Faithful Servant: That's just the point, wise, wonderful, omnipotent, omniscient, and omnipresent Master. They are going to need more than just smarts.

Creator: What do you have in mind, Faithful Servant?

Faithful Servant: Well, in order to solve all those problems, they will need a bit of flexibility in their smarts, a touch of originality, a pinch of inventiveness and independent thinking. Add imagination for spice and you've not only made gifted people, but creatively gifted people!

Creator: Bravo, Faithful Servant! Thank Go . . . er, me, for you. No, no, that's not right. Thank you for me. No, no, that's still not right. Good Lord, help me! No, no. Just forget it, Faithful Servant. Hand me the creativity jar.

All fantasy aside, our world is indeed facing serious problems. If we are to survive, it will be our gifted people who find solutions to these problems, and they will need all the things creativity is made of: innovative and original thinking; flexible, independent thinking; inventiveness and imagination. Creativity, like intelligence itself, is partially a product of heredity, but certainly environmental factors will play a part in its development. Parents of gifted children can create an atmosphere that both fosters and nurtures their child's creativity.

Many people mistakenly link intelligence and creativity together. While there has been some relationship between intelligence and creativity, it is not as close as some might imagine. Quite a few very gifted children have surprisingly small amounts of creativity, and this inevitably shows in the child's work, play, and interests. For example, the following are the work of Margaret and Zanti, both the same age, eight who both have roughly the same IQ score (150–155). When asked to write a poem, Margaret wrote:

Squiggly Worm

Squiggly wiggly worm
Went down the railroad track
Squiggly wiggly worm
Never really came back

We never really knew
What happened to squiggly worm
I think it was probably
Eaten by some big pachyderm

I know it is a story
Very sad to tell
And I hope he is alright
We all wish him well

Zanti wrote:

My Best Friend

My best friend
Is a very special person
She is very pretty
And she never fights.
And that is why
She is my best friend.

When asked what would make the world more perfect:

Margaret: For every person to be born with advanced minds. Then everybody would know all they need to know and we could make the right decisions for the future.
Zanti: If everyone got a hundred dollars.

When asked to write about their favorite trip over summer vacation:

Margaret: My favorite trip occurred when I fell off my bicycle and sprained my ankle. I had to stay in bed and so I took many trips to fairyland and faraway places, jungles, and had many fine adventures. All because the only thing I was allowed to do was read.

Zanti: My favorite trip was when my mother took me to my aunt's. It was a long trip because my aunt lives in the country. She has a lot of dogs and I played in the sprinklers and on the swings. My uncle put a quarter in my ear and said he found it, but I knew he was teasing. It was fun.

When asked how many words reminded them of the word *round*, Margaret named thirteen and Zanti named seven. When asked how many uses they could think of for a brick, Margaret came up with many original ideas, such as baseball bases, to build a fort or even a house, to throw at a monster, to crack open nuts, to make a road. Zanti said to build a house, a building, a fence, a yard, a schoolhouse, a fire station.

Finally, when asked what might have happened if Christopher Columbus had never discovered America, Margaret went into a lengthy, detailed account of what might have happened. Although her story was totally unfeasible, it was highly imaginative. Zanti, on the other hand, completely sidestepped the adventuresome question. Instead, she fell back to the area she was more comfortable in, that of relating the facts that she knew.

As you can see, there is a considerable difference between these two gifted children. Is this difference an innate one? Perhaps, but a look into each girl's family and personality type would indicate otherwise. The following is a brief montage taken from three different interviews with each girl's family.

Zanti is the only child of two college professors. Emphasis in the family is placed on academic performance and conformity. Zanti is very close to both her parents, especially her mother, and seems to have an exaggerated need to please adults.

Interviewer: What would you like your daughter to become as an adult?

Father: Well, considering Zanti's intelligence, I imagine she could do anything. I'd actually like to see her go to med school.

Mother: Yes, or into some other profession requiring an advanced degree.

Interviewer: What types of books do you read in the household?

Father: Mostly professional journals, with some other nonfiction on the side.

Mother: For me, just getting through the journals is quite a task. Every once in a while I'll indulge in some other book, usually nonfiction, also.

Interviewer: If Isaac Newton was born in a den of thieves, would he still have made the same accomplishments?

Mother: That's certainly a strange question.

Father: The fact is, Isaac Newton wasn't born in a pack of thieves. I don't see the relevancy of that question. What difference does it make?

Interviewer: (Bringing Zanti into the room) Could you show us how you would help Zanti do this math problem?

Father: Sure. (Looking over the problem) OK, Zanti, can you do this problem?

Zanti: No, I don't think so. We haven't got there in our math book.

Father: OK, look, there are many ways you can do this, but this is the best way to do it (shows Zanti). If you do it this way, you'll never be wrong; you'll always be right.

Interviewer: The last question. Could you briefly describe your child-rearing philosophy?

Father: We believe in providing a lot of structure and good old-fashioned discipline. Although Zanti's a good kid and she hardly ever needs it. She pretty much does what we want.

Mother: We try and always keep her busy with extra schoolwork. She needs that. We want her to have the best education possible.

Notice how Zanti's parents emphasize education as a means to the professions that offer considerable status, social acceptability, and security. There is a right way and a wrong way to do problems. Her parents rarely step outside the hard facts or reality, as shown through their reading material and their unwillingness to even consider the hypothetical question concerning Isaac Newton. Contrast these answers to the answers of Margaret's parents. Her father is an engineer and her mother is a nurse; Margaret is the youngest of three children.

Interviewer: What would you like your daughter to become as an adult?

Father: Healthy and satisfied with her work. I think those are the two most important issues that affect overall happiness.

Mother: Yes, of course, we want her to be healthy and happy. And, of course, she is going to become whatever she wants. If I were going to put a condition on it, I'd like her to have work that always remains a challenge, that's exciting and something she finds worthwhile.

Father: I'll agree with that.

Interviewer: If Isaac Newton was born in a pack of thieves, would he have accomplished as much?

Father: That's a surprising question, interesting though.

Mother: Yes, the age-old question of whether or not our behavior's predetermined or predestined, and how much our environment controls us.

Father: I've always felt very strongly that . . . (they discussed this question for over fifteen minutes).

Interviewer: What type of books do you like to read?

Father: Oh no, you're going to hear from my wife on this one! (laughter) She tends to read great literature. I've been through periods where I've read good books, but lately I've been into popular books. I read a lot of science fiction, adventure novels, etc. You know, fast-paced, first-class junk.

Mother: He is the king of the paperbacks. He reads about one every two days. I prefer the great classics, myself.

Interviewer: (Bringing Margaret in) Could you help Margaret do this math problem?

Father: Margaret, you can do this by yourself, can't you, honey?

Margaret: I think so. (She struggles for about five minutes and finally her mother interrupts.)

Mother: You really have to think on this one. I'll give you a hint. There are four ways, maybe more, that you can do it, but they all have to do with finding the right multiple of this number.

Margaret: Oh, I get it!

Father: Can you do it any other way?

Interviewer: Can you briefly describe your child-rearing philosophy?

Father: A child-rearing philosophy? You mean the way we raise Margaret?

Mother: Not in twenty-five words or less! Just lots of love and room to grow in.

Father: And we try and expose her to a lot of different things, get her interested in things. Is that what you mean? We don't have to do much parenting with Margaret, she is already a fine person.

Margaret's parents are concerned with allowing their child to unfold as she will, and they seem to stress individuality more than Zanti's parents. They are also more capable of diving outside the "concrete" reality and into the world of fantasy and imagination, the world of what might have happened.

Certainly parents have some effect on their children's creative potential. It seems that the landscape of creativity can become barren: when order and cleanliness exceeds comfort and ease; when parents stress conformity and submissiveness over individuality and independence; when the right way is always better than the child's way; when the child turns to the parent instead of to him/herself to know what is pleasing; and when the child is certain of right and wrong, good and bad, black and white, truth and lies, fantasy and fact. These things are obvious. What is not as obvious are the things a parent can do to foster and encourage creativity in their children.

First, encouraging creativity in your children starts by behaving creatively yourself. Children who witness their parents' creativity are more likely to feel comfortable with their own creative expression. "Fine," you say, "but how do you get those creative juices flowing?" or, more appropriate, "Just exactly what do you mean?"

Perhaps the following questions will shed light on possible ways that a parent can model creativity:

1. Do you listen to a variety of music? Do you share this with your child?
2. Do you always prepare the same foods? Do you ever experiment with dinner? Create your own recipes?
3. Does your life fit neatly into a series of routines? Do you know what your spouse will say to you after work? Do you have a particular day, time, pattern for mowing the lawn, washing the car, taking a shower? Does your dog know the exact time he will go for a walk?
4. Are you ever eccentric?
5. Is each weekend filled with the same old activities? Are these activities done with the same old friends?
6. Do you ever fantasize? Do you ever share these fantasies, hopes, dreams with your family?
7. Have you ever insisted that the whole family join you for a walk in the rain?
8. Do you often find yourself discussing breakthroughs in science? Different political ideologies? That book you just finished, or that movie you just saw?
9. Would you ever consider allowing a wall in your house to be turned into a family mural?
10. Are all your shoes brown?

The point is that children learn from watching their parents. They can learn that there is a narrow range of acceptable behavior; a narrow range of acceptable ways of just being. Or the child's eyes can be opened to the number of infinite possibilities life has to offer.

There is a variety of direct ways to spur the gifted child's creative thinking. The following is a list of discussion topics and activities related to the broad subjects of science, language, philosophy, history, and social science. Most of these questions are appropriate for children of all ages. This list is by no means inclusive, and parents are sure to find that they can generate their own ideas, questions, and activities that help a child think creatively.

It is also important to note before beginning that the purpose of each question is not to find the right answer, but rather to train flexibility of thought. Some children will undoubtedly discover the right answer in their exploration of each question, but always the emphasis should be on the multiplicity of answers, possible explanations, and "truths." For this reason, the following guidelines will be helpful:

1. After each question and answer ask, "What other possibilities, reasons, etc., can you think of?
2. No criticism is allowed. This is particularly important if you are discussing these questions with the whole family or a group. In general, try to steer clear of any atmosphere where the child feels like he/she is being tested or judged.
3. Reward the number of ideas the child has; in other words, go for quantity, not quality.
4. All ideas are acceptable, no matter how farfetched they seem.
5. Save any discussion of specific ideas for after all possibilities are exhausted.

Science

1. Can you name all the things we burn in the house?
2. Place a handful or more of marbles on the floor. Have the

child walk on top of the marbles. Ask why it is hard to walk on top of marbles. (If the child responds with "because they're round," ask why it's hard to walk on something that's round.)

3. Twist a lid tightly onto a jar. Have the child try to open it. Place the jar under hot water and have the child try. Ask why the jar is easy to open after running hot water on it.

4. Why don't light bulbs burn up?

5. Fill a paper cup half full with water. Set the top of the cup on fire (in a safe place) and watch the fire burn down to the water level. Ask why no water spilled. Can you think of other possibilities?

6. Why do helium balloons rise?

7. What makes airplanes fly?

8. Put a metal spoon and a wooden spoon in boiling water. Ask why one gets hot and the other doesn't.

9. What makes sound come from the radio? The phone? (These will be more difficult for the younger child. However, the purpose is not to ascertain the "right answer," but to teach the child to explore possibilities.)

10. Take a spool of thread, a ruler and some other object to make a lever. Ask why a lever makes it easier to lift something. Ask the child to find all the levers in the house.

11. Why do soaps work? Medicines? Vitamins?

12. Fill three pans with water at hot, cold, and medium temperatures. Have the child place one hand in hot, the other in cold for a minute. Then have the child place both hands in the medium water. What happens? Why?

13. What do seeds eat?

14. What makes plants grow?

15. What makes your stomach growl?

16. What makes you sleepy? Thirsty? etc.

17. How do your eyes work? Your ears? Your taste buds, your nose? Your sense of touch?

18. Take the child's temperature and then check the temperature of the room. Why are they different?

19. Name all the uses you can think of for a newspaper, knife, cork, shoe, button, key, chair, tin can, etc.

As you can see, there are endless numbers of questions that can help your child to learn to explore the environment and science while training creative, flexible thinking.

Social Science and History

Once again, the goal of this section is to stimulate the child's thinking, not to find the right answer. Therefore, most of the discussions will center on possibilities, not on "facts." This will teach the child to probe beyond the facts, to explore beyond the obvious.

What might have happened if ...? This question can be applied to any part of history the child might be studying. For instance:

1. What might have happened if Lincoln lived?
2. If the British won the Revolutionary War?
3. If the South seceded from the Union?
4. If Germany and Japan won World War II?
5. If the Louisiana Territory remained French?
6. If Spain held the western portion of the United States?
7. If the Russian revolution failed?
8. If the Chinese revolution failed?

You can see the possibilities here; they are, in fact, endless. You might also want to broaden the nature of these questions, for instance:

9. If Ireland held all the world's oil supplies? Or Israel?
10. If the middle United States was desert?
11. If England was attached to Europe?
12. If Japan was attached to China?
13. If the United States was on the equator?

14. If we could understand the language of animals and birds?
15. If there was a hole through the earth?
16. If we could become invisible?
17. If there were no racial differences between people?

In another realm, you can ask what are the possible reasons for:

18. The Civil War? World War II? Vietnam War? etc.
19. Why England has a king and the United States doesn't?
20. Why China built the Great Wall?
21. Why Egypt built the Pyramids?
22. Why people colonized from Europe?
23. Why third world countries are poor?

And what would you do if:

24. You were president of the United States?
25. If you were the party leader in Russia?
26. President of Mexico?
27. Principal of your school? Teacher of your class?
28. Head of an oil company? The Environmental Protection Agency? In charge of seeing that animals are cared for?

Philosophy

As in the social science and science section, parents will want to probe for as many answers as possible here.

1. How do you know what's real?
   a. How do you know it's real if you haven't ever viewed it, smelled it, felt it, heard it, tasted it?
   b. How do you know $2 + 2 = 4$?
      How do you know the table is real? Yourself? Other people?
2. What is the best way to treat people? Why and how do you know? Why do people treat others badly? Are all people equal?

3. How did the universe (or God) get here?
4. What happens when something dies? What is the difference between something that's dead and something that's alive?
5. What makes something beautiful and something else ugly?
6. What if you are the only person that's real?
7. What rights do people have? Animals? Children?
8. Create a story where the main character has had an awful, tragic life and then does something criminal because of it. Ask the child if that person is really responsible for his/her actions. Contrast this story with the opposite, a person who has everything and every opportunity and does something great.

Language, the Arts, and Imagination

In this section, it is important not to be judgmental. The child should be completely free of the burden of possible failure, and all efforts need to be encouraged.

1. Make up an ending for this poem. (Parents should provide beginning.) Make up as many possible endings as you can for this poem.
2. Write a story about . . . Parents can generate topics, but try to keep the topics as nonspecific as possible. For instance, ages six through ten will enjoy:
   The dog that doesn't bark
   The woman who can but won't talk
   The rooster that doesn't crow
   The girl who wants to play soccer
   The boy who wants to be a nurse
   The cupboard that ate the cookies
   The monkey that flew
   The lion that won't roar
3. Words:
   a. Name all the words that rhyme with . . .
   b. Name all the other word that mean . . .
   c. Name all the words that mean the opposite of . . .

     d. Name all the words that come to your head when I say . . .
     e. Name all the words that start with the prefix . . .
     f. Name all the words that end with . . .
4. Write a story about this picture.
5. Use a sheet of paper and ask the child to pictorially represent as many words as he can think of—tall, fat, etc.
6. Draw or paint any experience you have had.
7. Create visual impressions of music; try many different kinds. (The great variety of classical music is good for this purpose.)
8. How does this picture make you feel?
9. Draw an angry, sad, happy, bored, etc. bird, elephant, circle, tree, person (emphasize the use of color).
10. Allow the child to draw and then paint a mural (on his/her bedroom wall). If this is impractical, have child use a large piece of paper.
11. Draw an animal that reminds you of this music.
12. Sculpt an animal that reminds you of this music.
13. Make a pot that you've never seen before.
14. Create a figure that you've never seen before from this clay.

Hopefully, these questions and activities will provide parents with an understanding of how to spur the child's creativity and imagination and flexibility of thought. And this profound task can be done in the most mundane situations—during dinner, while driving in the car, or while washing the dishes. It is easy to do and can be fun and stimulating for both parent and child.

THE DEVELOPMENT OF CREATIVE AND ARTISTIC TALENT

Great Creator: So now we have creatively gifted people. I find it hard to imagine that I—the great one—forgot about all the talented artists who are to walk the pages of my book of life. Imagine, my planet devoid of all its paintings, sculptures, and books and poems and, oh my . . . imagine a world without music!

Faithful Servant: But wise and noble, great and nice Creator, just because you've added creativity to giftedness doesn't mean you'll get talented artists.

Great Creator: Faithful Servant, are you trying to tell me—me, the great, omnipotent, omniscient, perhaps even omnipresent one—that I forgot something again! (angry volcanoes begin erupting on the earth's surface).

Faithful Servant: Oh no, Great Creator, let me explain. Artistic talent is a mix of many ingredients, many of which you play no part in. The kids must have more than general intelligence, sensitivity, imagination, and the ability to arrive at new ideas and values. They must also express an early interest in their field, they need early opportunity, encouragement, guidance, and instruction. All these ingredients combine so that the kids are first able to master the medium. And these ingredients manifest from the time, place, and the general environment that the kids grow up in. Why, do you remember Mozart, who appears in the eighteenth century?

Great Creator: Ah yes, the little devil who they said transmitted my voice through his music.

Faithful Servant: (Under his breath) I wish you could speak so well.

Great Creator: What was that, Faithful Servant? I didn't quite hear you.

Faithful Servant: I was just saying I read that if Mozart lived in the twentieth century instead of the eighteenth, then he would have probably never composed. Instead, he might have become a quarterback for the New York Jets or something.

Great Creator: I don't get your point, Faithful Servant. I can't very well put eighteenth-century Vienna into the batch, can I?

Faithful Servant: No, and that is the point, My Lord, the kid must have an environment that nurtures the talent you give him, or it's no deal.

Great Creator: But that means I have to leave it up to chance! How can I do that when I don't even believe in chance?

Faithful Servant: I'm sure you'll figure something out.

Of course, Faithful Servant is right. Artistic talent depends on many factors, only two of which are giftedness and creativity. Gifted artists in any field—visual arts, music, choreography, dancing, writing, or acting must be dedicated to their art far beyond what most of us can even imagine. No matter how gifted or creative, few children will demonstrate the necessary motivation to excel in an artistic field. The rare child who has both the talent and the desire must also have an opportunity to pursue the art and an environment that encourages this pursuit. Considering the factors that go into art, the richness of the world is truly astounding.

However, every child should be exposed to some aspects of the "arts," and children will benefit in many ways from any exposure to the arts. Perhaps most important, exposure cultivates appreciation and understanding. Art does not mean as much as if we are only able to view the end product—hear the symphony played, see the play or ballet being performed, or look at the finished canvas on the wall. We need a glimpse into the process of creating the art before we can fully appreciate this end product. Therefore, parents of gifted children will want to allow their children to choose one or more of the artistic areas.

Many parents might question just how much "encouragement" a child needs to explore art. In other words, some parents ponder, "To shove or not to shove a piano down Johnny's throat." Two different experiences demonstrate this argument.

I've always been glad my parents made me take piano lessons. They wanted me to end up doing it professionally, but unfortunately, I was not quite good enough, a near miss. Still, I play often, it is my joy in life and a rewarding hobby. I don't like to think of what might have happened if they ever allowed me to stop playing. And there were many times that I begged them to do just that; I had other things to do—more important things, like watching TV and painting my nails, chatting with a friend, and so on.

My parents made me take piano lessons until I was fifteen, and then they finally gave up. I have always hated it; now, after all those years of hard time put in, I don't even want to *hear* a piano, let alone play one! I would never do that to my kids.

In general, it seems best to allow each child to choose what activity is interesting and exciting, and how much effort to spend on it. As with most things, parents will need to strike a balance between force and freedom. Too much force will create the impression that the activity is a chore and, like most chores, will be best avoided. On the other hand, complete freedom often means the child expends no effort at all. Most parents will find that simple encouragement, rewards, and showing an interest in the child's activity are enough to motivate the pursuit.

In summary, the ingredients necessary to help your gifted child become more creative are:

1. A little creativity demonstrated by the parents of the child.
2. Attempts to point out the creativity that already abounds in our society.
3. Teaching the child to explore beyond the obvious answers, past the facts and the right answers and into the wonderful world of the imagination, the possible, the "what if."
4. Encouraging the child's exploration of the creative arts, for art's sake alone.

Chapter 4
Toward Mental Health

PART I—THE SOCIAL ARENA

MANY YOUNG GIFTED CHILDREN MANAGE TO THRIVE IN THE social arena. Fueled by intelligence, these children often demonstrate amazing organizational and leadership abilities. Their talents and charm evoke admiration, likability, and respect from peers, family, and adults alike. They, too, like other people; this allows them to be successful in each social network they encounter.

Unfortunately, not all gifted children are successful in the social realm, and research demonstrates that if a gifted child is to have trouble in life, it is likely that the trouble will be in the social arena. Some gifted children come to feel different and often alienated from the mainstream. This real or perceived difference from others can cause shyness, introversion and lack of self-confidence, inadequate development of social skills, aggressive and dominating behavior, or the development of a megalomaniacal personality. Parents will need to first examine these personality patterns and then explore the ways in which these problems can be prevented or eliminated.

The first of the social problems that gifted children are prone to is the domineering personality. One father describes how his son developed this personality characteristic:

I don't know what happened to my boy. Kurt is eight now, and it really looks like we have a problem. I think it started when we began realizing just how smart he is (IQ 160+). My wife and I were so proud, so anxious to encourage him, that I guess we overdid it. He has the impression that he can do anything and that he is very special. He seems to take great pains to assert his superiority over other kids. Frankly, he is arrogant, bossy, and even somewhat of a bully. He is so damned manipulative. Why, whenever we, his parents, reprimand his bullying behavior, he comes back with, "Don't blame me! You're the ones who raised me!" He has few friends left and does he care? No way; as he said, "They were just dumb, anyway."

Similar to the domineering, manipulative gifted child is the megalomaniacal child:

I never thought I'd say this, but I'm actually afraid of my own daughter, Clair. Yes, she is exceptionally gifted, and that is the problem. She has realized she is better than other people. She is more capable, quick-witted, and competent than others. Her learning and memory speed alone would scare most people. She will actually test people on their intelligence and draw harsh judgments on this basis. She even tests her friends. Needless to say, she has few. Once she actually said to me, "You know, it is very difficult to be surrounded by such dummies." And I just cringe when she asks me a question that I don't know the answer to. The look of contempt she gives me is enough to tingle the spine. Of course I've taken her to a psychologist, but she didn't respect him either.

Obviously, these children have developed a dangerous problem. Some authority figure (usually a parent or a teacher) has convinced the child that he/she is very special, perhaps even superior to others. The child soon notices that, indeed, he/she can think better, quicker, easier than others. Messages (subtle and otherwise) and reinforcement begin to affirm their superiority and all too soon, a vicious cycle is set into motion.

These children start justifying their behavior on the basis that they are superior to others. They can even go so far as to separate the world into two distinct groups: those who are as smart, and those who aren't. They are right; others are wrong. Obviously, this type of elitism alienates friends, teachers, and even parents. The gifted young child may believe that the cause of his alienation is that other people can't understand or recognize his giftedness and that perhaps other people are just jealous. The alienation can thus actually reinforce the belief that the child is superior.

The alienation viciously feeds on itself, creating impenetrable barriers between people. The barriers do offer protection for the inflated self-image, but ultimately, reality intrudes. Feelings of loneliness, self-doubt, being unloved creep in and trigger depression. In a desperate attempt to deal with the negative feelings, most of these people eventually inflate their self-image even more. These are sad people, endlessly tangled in a most vicious cycle.

The third and most common social problem among gifted children is verboseness. Gifted children tend to express every thought in both great detail and in a rapid-fire manner. These children frequently overwhelm others with the extent of their expressiveness. They become verbal to a fault and soon lose all interactive abilities found in healthy communication. One teacher of gifted children relates his experience:

I've taught gifted children for ten years. Most of these kids are extremely verbal; they talk endlessly and go into great detail about everything. This is fine, for the most part. It only becomes a problem if the kid begins lengthy monologues and stops interacting, stops allowing others a turn to talk. The worst case of this was this one girl, Stephanie. She was a talker. She would go nonstop if you let her, and it seemed her parents did. Pretty soon I began noticing that she wasn't listening to anyone. She would start talking, and if you commented on what she said, she would continue as though you never said anything, right where she left off. I wish I had paid more attention to this, for I later found out that by the time she was seventeen the problem was so bad and so crazy that she was institutionalized.

The last social problem that gifted children often develop is a form of shyness, which is really the lack of desire to interact with other children. Thomas was such a child:

I have the most quiet, shy child you ever saw. Thomas hardly ever says a word; he buries himself in books. He seems to have no friends. His father and I ask him questions constantly and he replies with a "yes," "no," "I dunno," or a minimum of words. The funny thing is that we know there is a lot going on because we had him tested and he is exceptionally gifted (from his father's side of the family, certainly not from my side). But from raising him, one would get the impression that he is dull. There is just no way to reach him.

Research has demonstrated that most gifted children are even less assertive (socially adept) than other children, and that the greatest problem area for gifted children is that of inadequate social skills. Unfortunately, gifted children may suffer greatly from this single factor alone. People with college degrees (and most mentally gifted adults fall in this category) have a higher-than-average divorce rate and an overall higher dissatisfaction with marriage. These adults also report that they feel greater unhappiness and dissatisfaction with life in general. Obviously, part of these problems are caused by the greater expectations gifted people have. However, these problems are largely related to the gifted person's lower assertion skills.

Perhaps most disturbing of all is that the lack of social skills relates directly to unrealized career potential. Many less-gifted adults become more successful in careers simply because they know how to "play the game," they know how to present a better self-image, and they are able to weave through the company's or institution's social networks. Some gifted people never learn to stand up for themselves, and, therefore, many of their ideas, innovations, or problem-solving abilities are credited to others. The following two stories illustrate this rather common experience.

I'm a management consultant for electronic firms. I'm hired by a company to rearrange things in a more productive manner. This not only includes changing the organizational structure of the company, but also hiring, firing, and promoting personnel. After being in this kind of work for fifteen years, I've gotten very good at spotting one problem that never ceases to amaze me: Very often the best, brightest, most capable individuals go completely unnoticed. They remain in lower-level positions and are never considered for promotions. Certainly the individual's assertiveness is in question here, but more to the point, these individuals almost always lose credit for their work, ideas, innovations, etc. They passively allow other people to take their credit, to run them down. Not only does this occur at a high cost to the individual, but also to the company itself.

Another story:

I've just started doing industrial consulting and frankly, I'm amazed at the problems involved. Last week I was sitting in on a particularly stressful decision-making session on top management personnel. The president asked for discussion, ideas, suggestions, and right away you could see a hierarchy develop. First the president, followed by two vice-presidents, and so on. Well, this one man at the low end of the totem pole suggested a solution. The vice-president immediately saw this solution's worth and discussed it further. The president became convinced, and before long everyone was talking about the benefits. At this point, I stopped the procedure and asked everyone to write down whose idea it was. All twelve people, with the exception of the vice-president, *including the man whose idea it was*, thought that it was the vice-president's idea! Furthermore, the president was going to give the vice-president a raise for it! The vice-president (being a good sort) laughed and gave the credit to whom it belonged. Everyone was surprised. This incident just shows how the passive (or less aggressive) individual often gets the short end of the deal.

As you can see, huge costs can result from the gifted child's inability to deal successfully with social situations. Problems that gifted children have in developing social skills are the result of two phenomena: First, people tend to avoid things that they are not good at and seek things that they are good at. Gifted children are encouraged to pursue intellectual and scholarly interests, and, frequently, these interests bring them the most enjoyment. Secondly, as mentioned previously, gifted children often do feel different, sometimes alienated from others. Even the development of megalomania is largely a response to social insecurities or an overcompensation for inadequacies. Fortunately, assertion training, along with empathy and egalitarian training, can greatly enhance the gifted child's social skills.

Obviously, under certain conditions any child is capable of developing these traits. However, the mentally gifted child is particularly susceptible to developing these maladaptive personality patterns. Parents will want to take extra precautions to prevent (or eliminate) these problems. The first step is to teach egalitarian and democratic principles.

Teaching egalitarian and democratic principles simply means showing children that they are only part of the whole. It means teaching children to share, take turns, and work well in group situations, the goal being that the child will learn to find the worth of each individual and the important balance between individual striving and group cooperation. These are unquestionably important lessons.

Children learn egalitarian and democratic principles through parental modeling of these attitudes. The power of parental modeling on a child's behavior is truly amazing. It seems children are at all times watching parents interact and respond in the many different situations life presents. The intensely curious child is even more aware of and able to comprehend the many subtle cues and suggestions that are present in a parent's behavior.

Family situations offer an excellent medium for the teaching of these principles. Whenever possible, include the entire family in a decision-making process. Ask each member to offer opinions; encourage discussion of each point brought up. For decisions that are strictly a matter of personal selection (such as where to go for dinner or what to have for dinner), rotate the decision through the family. For instance, tonight Mom chooses, next week you get to choose. The more frequently a family can model reciprocity, the more a child will understand the democratic process of groups.

Parents can also present egalitarian principles in action simply by showing respect to all people and by interacting with as many different kinds of people as possible. Church and temple services and meetings, along with community-sponsored activities and meetings, usually offer excellent opportunities to meet a variety of different people. It also benefits children to allow them to join in any political involvements of their parents.

Many games offer a means of stressing democratic principles. All games that require reciprocity or the taking of turns are good for this purpose. Monopoly, chess, Scrabble, card games, and most other games fall in this category. Furthermore, all team sports that require cooperation and emphasize the group effort—such as basketball, football, soccer, and the like—are worthwhile. Special interest clubs, such as Boy or Girl Scouts and hobby clubs, are good democratic training grounds. These activities will enhance your child's ability to participate in group settings.

Parents will also want to examine the messages the gifted child receives about giftedness. Many parents of gifted children unintentionally create grandiose or inflated self-images in their children by overemphasizing the child's giftedness. These parents manage to reinforce an idea that not only is the child very special, but that this specialness is a license to behave in non-democratic ways. The child receives considerable attention for giftedness; giftedness is always mentioned, is always an issue. In this way, the parents' attitude toward giftedness serves as a fuel for megalomania.

Another mistake parents of gifted children make is to excuse antisocial behavior on a basis that the child is gifted. Some parents excuse or ignore even the most obnoxious behavior for this reason. This attitude at the very least leads to elitism, and at worst to sociopathology (the tendency to hurt other people without feeling any guilt or remorse). One mother's experience illustrates this:

I met Carolyn when she started working as a nurse in the hospital where I'm an administrator. One of the first things I knew about her was how brilliant her son Charles was. Carolyn constantly managed to bring the topic up. Well, we got to be friends, having many similar interests. One day I remember we took our kids to the museum and park. We were buying some lunch at a concession stand when all of a sudden the man behind the counter started yelling at Charles to put something back before he called the police. It turned out that Charles had taken a little red flag and a candy bar and put them in his pocket! Do you know what Carolyn said? She said, "Oh, Charles does things like that to see if he can get away with it. He is just more curious than other kids, he has to try everything out." That's all, no punishment or anything.

There is really no behavior that should be excused because a child is gifted. Parents should make certain that they treat the gifted child like all others. Parents should (and can) expect fair play and consideration of others from the gifted child. To do otherwise can create dangerous and pathological consequences.

Many gifted children need help in developing appropriate conversation skills. These skills consist of learning the balance between talking and listening to others. Mastering conversation skills helps children to become more likable people and teaches children to shift their focus from themselves to others. Life is certain to become richer when a person can reach out to others.

Teaching conversation skills is both easy and fun. Start by making conversation into a "my turn—your turn" game. The child takes the first turn by making a statement or comment or relating an observation about something. The parent then takes a turn, but must ask a question concerning the child's information. Only after the child answers the question can the parent then take a turn, making his own statement, comment, or observation. The child must then ask a question concerning the parent's information. The following is a sample dialogue:

Child: I think Carey is my best friend.
Parent: Why do you like about Carey?

Child: Well, he likes everything I like and well, he's funny. We can act silly together.

Parent: I remember I had a friend like Carey when I was your age. Her name was Pam.

Child: What did you like about Pam?

Parent: Oh, that we shared so much together, like you and Carey. What sorts of silly things do you and Carey do?

For the young child, parents will want to simplify this game into just "my turn—your turn." You will be surprised at how quickly your child learns both listening skills and interaction skills from this game. In addition, this is good training for the shy child.

Parents will also want to discourage their children from interrupting when others are speaking. Gifted children seem to interrupt more frequently than others. Bright children usually have more to contribute to a conversation and their minds also tend to race ahead of normal conversation speed. Discourage interrupting gently by simply pointing out that interrupting is unfair and is not allowed.

Empathy Training

Some gifted children feel separate or different from others. These feelings can cause problems, especially in a world that insists on conformity and similarity between people. In extreme cases, gifted children have felt isolated and depressed because of their differences. They are too young to understand that each person is a unique individual, different from others in different ways, and that being exceptionally smart is an asset in our world instead of a deficit.

Empathy training helps children in this area. Empathy training teaches children to understand others, to feel compassion for others, and sometimes even to feel what someone else is feeling. These abilities ease the feeling of being separated and different.

Understanding and compassion of others will, instead, connect the gifted child to people.

Parents can teach children to be empathetic. Of course, children will first learn this by watching their parents respond empathetically. This means that the child sees the parent attend to the feelings and problems of others. For instance, an empathetic parent might discreetly point out a "skid row drunk" and comment, "Isn't it sad when people have so many problems or life becomes so overwhelming that they can't cope?" Or the empathetic parent might comment at the end of a sporting event, "Boy, isn't it great to win. They must be so excited and happy!" The child learns to watch for the emotional state of people.

There are many other things a parent might do to cultivate a child's empathetic responses. The following are four games that help children understand and feel compassion for others.

1. The Other Side

Gifted children often need to learn to adopt another person's point of view. A bright child is able to sort and process information and draw conclusions quicker than others. These children tend to be rather rigid and dogmatic in their conclusions and, therefore, often make harsher judgments. For instance, Shelly, a seven-year-old gifted child, became morally outraged when her teacher reprimanded the entire class for being noisy when she was quietly reading at her desk. Shelly thought the teacher was being very unfair and, furthermore, that the teacher owed her an apology. When the teacher heard Shelly's complaint (and request), she almost laughed. Shelly concluded that the teacher wasn't worthy of minding anymore. Obviously, this attitude is a bit rigid. These children need to see the many shades of gray instead of the simplistic black or white.

Parents will find that playing The Other Side shows the child another person's point of view. The game can be played whenever the child states an opinion, criticizes someone, or takes a position on an issue. Ask the child to pretend to be the other person and to ask questions similar to these: Would your opinion or feelings change? How would they be different? How might you justify their position? What reasoning would another person use? and so forth. For example, Shelly's parent might have asked her to pretend she was a teacher who had a noisy class. What would you do? Or why do you think your teacher did what she did?

Parents might find that some children will ardently resist adopting another person's point of view. However, gentle probing is certain to push their minds into action. Remember that the purpose of this game is not to change the child's mind (even though this might be the result). Instead, it should provide the child with an understanding of someone else's point of view.

You are likely to find many daily opportunities to play The Other Side. Sibling arguments, arguments with friends, conflicts with a teacher will all provide good starting points for this game. Parents might also want to play this game when explaining or discussing history. For instance, one parent explains how this game works for his ten-year-old son, Craig:

Craig is so smart that he finds fault with everything and everyone. There is a wrong way and then there is Craig's way. On the advice of my therapist I started playing this game with him, The Other Side. At first he couldn't (or wouldn't) see another person's point of view. Then I decided to make it worth his while. I gave him a quarter toward a chemistry set he wanted every time he could give me five reasons from another person's point of view (one that's different from his). At first he had great difficulty even when he was highly motivated. Now he is much better, and I can even sense a change of personality in him.

---

2. "How Would You Feel if...?

This game is just a slight variation of The Other Side. The game can be played anytime, anywhere, by simply asking children, "How would you feel if you were a Pilgrim, a colonist, an Indian, your sister, your father, your teacher, a ballet dancer, a dolphin, a policeman, etc?" As you can see, this game involves countless possibilities for children to explore what life (or a situation) would be like if they were another person or thing. Once again, this game simply shifts a child's focus from self to others.

3. The Reading Game

A child's reading often offers excellent opportunities for empathy training. Ask your child to relate in detail the book he/she has read. Ask the child to describe the characters, the plot, and the conflict. What character does he like best, least, and why? What would he do if he were the main character? Who is the antagonist and why is this person or group doing what they are doing? Parents will also want to give opinions or comments. Always try to lead the child to insights into a character's motivation and feelings and provide sympathy for the character's situation. For instance, a parent might comment on a character motivated by greed, "It is horrible when a person thinks only of money. I always feel sorry for people like that. They end up missing so much." These kinds of discussions are certain to soften a child's harsher judgments and ease away dogmatism.

4. Underdog Training

In almost every school there are children who are virtually friendless—in other words, outcasts. The daily reminders of this painful childhood isolation serves to strengthen the barrier between themselves and others. Over any period of time, this "isolation barrier" creates even greater personal tragedy. One child who offers these children friendship can change this unfortunate situation.

Underdog training teaches your child to befriend one of these children. Not only will this help the friendless child, but your child will also benefit in many ways. Hopefully, your child will learn both to sympathize with the less fortunate and to take an active role in helping others. Perhaps best of all, your child can develop a new and worthwhile friendship.

Underdog training starts by asking your child if there is any person at school who is friendless. Ask your child to relate both what he/she knows about this person and how he/she feels about this person. Good questions would be similar to, "Why do you think this person has no friends?" "Why do you think he/she is like that?" "How would you feel if you had no friends?" Discuss the situation at great length.

Most children will conclude that there is something different or unusual about the isolated child. The difference often involves dress, appearance, and, less frequently, strange behavior. For instance, one child explained, "Well, she isolates herself. She is from India and she dresses funny and talks differently." At this point you will want to discuss differences among people and how both important and unimportant these differences are. Take care to emphasize that we are all different from each other in some ways and that differences are worthwhile to explore.

Next, ask your child if there is something nice that he/she might do for this child. This nice thing can be anything from offering a compliment, insisting he join a game, picking her for a team, asking him to play after school, joining her for lunch, starting a conversation, or simply saying "hello." Ask your child to do one nice thing for this person each day. Make the whole endeavor a secret between you and your child, and be sure to support the child's efforts with a hug, kiss, or praise. One mother explains how her ten-year-old daughter, Cecila, befriended an otherwise friendless girl at school:

My daughter came home from school one day and told me a story that just broke my heart. Apparently there was a new girl in school from Japan. Cecila explained how this girl looked and dressed differently and was hardly able to speak English. Cecila went on to explain that the other kids made fun of her to a point that she started crying and wanted to go home. Kids can be so cruel. We talked about how difficult it must be for her in a strange country and I told her about the year I spent in France studying literature. I asked my daughter to be especially nice to her and to try and become friends. She agreed and each day thereafter she would come home and tell me about something nice she did for Kimberly. Well, eventually they became best friends, and after two years, I can't tell you how much Cecila has learned from this experience.

A slight variation on the underdog training theme is the be-nice-to-_____day. Just pick one day a week on which you and your child are especially nice to a person. The person can be anyone—a neighbor, friend, sibling, parent, or teacher. At the end of the day you can discuss how successfully the program worked.

The Shy Gifted Child
Some gifted children are shy and unskilled socially. The following stories describe the most common causes for gifted children to develop shyness:

My son Kevin is only interested in mathematics. I guess that's why he is so shy with other kids. No, he doesn't have any friends, but he doesn't want any, either. He has nothing in common with them.

June, my nine-year-old, prefers the company of adults. Her not having any friends worries me sometimes, but she is awfully mature for her age. She always says that she is just not interested in what kids her age are interested in.

My twelve-year-old is just interested in computers. He already has a job with a firm! Anyway, I worry. He has no friends or other interests. He is totally focused on this one thing. Around people, he blends imperceptibly into the walls, so shy and withdrawn.

Children need to interact with others, for unlike an amoeba, a shark, or even a cat, human beings are social creatures. Children learn about themselves and others through interacting. And eventually children come to know the joy of intimacy that is found via our connections with others. People are important to our success in life.

What can a parent do to reverse the shy script of a child?

Plenty. First, parents should refuse to abnegate their control over their children. You can force your child to interact with others. All a parent needs to do is pick an object or activity that the child values and then make the obtaining of that object or activity conditional on the child's socializing with others. For instance, exchange a desired book, that quiet block of time for study, that chemistry set, or that new bike—whatever your child truly wants—for participation one day a week in some group activity. The group activity can be anything from Scouts, team sports activities, choir, group skating lessons, a children's theater group—anything that will force the child into a social setting. Parents are likely to find that despite initial protestations, the child comes to enjoy the social activity. One mother of a gifted child explains how this worked for her daughter:

My daughter Shelly was only interested in one thing, primates—actually, monkeys. She wanted to be a vet who specialized in monkeys! All she ever read about was animals, and she did this full time. She was so introverted, I just couldn't see allowing it. So, one day I told her she had to pick one night a week to take some kind of lessons. She could pick the lessons. Reluctantly (I won't tell you how much she objected to this new rule) she picked ice-skating. The first time we went she turned to me and said, "Oh mother, I simply cannot do that. I'm sure I'll make a fool of myself." At first she dreaded it, but skating has grown on her. Now, she goes maybe three or four times a week with two other girls she met there. They are beginning to do other things together as well—shows, shopping, etc. It has really worked.

Parents will want to increase the shy child's verbal interaction. Many parents complain that they will ask the child questions only to be continually answered with a simple, *yes, no, fine, OK*. "How was your day today?" "Fine." "Anything unusual happen? "No." "Did your teacher comment on your paper?" "No," and so forth. The solution to this dilemma is to ask open questions—questions that cannot be answered with a *yes, no, fine*, or *OK*. For instance, "What did you do in school today?" "What is that book about; will you share the plot with me?" "What do you like about your teacher?" "What don't you like about your teacher?" Ask the child to share information on anything and everything in his/her life. These types of questions will force the shy child to open up more to you.

Shy children will often need gentle instruction on appropriate body language. Make certain that the child looks others in the eye when talking, and that facial expressions are appropriate for what is being said. You might also want to demonstrate the power of touch when you are talking. Show the child that if he/she reaches out and lightly touches the person while speaking, the message becomes more powerful.

Always be certain to encourage any conversation in which the child participates. Reach over with a hug, kiss, or pat on the shoulder after a conversation. You might like to comment or praise the child with statements similar to, "I sure enjoy it when you start opening up!" or "You make a very good impression when you start talking." Try to maintain this positive air in order to encourage the child.

Assertion and Self-Confidence Training

Shy and socially unskilled gifted children will also need a rigorous program of assertion training. Assertion training teaches children how to deal directly and honestly with people. Assertive children know how to interact successfully in social situations, how to initiate interaction, how to make requests and refusals, how to compliment and criticize, and, basically, how to get what they want. This training is helpful for all children, but it is imperative for shy, introverted gifted children.

The first step in assertion training is to teach your children how to make direct requests. An assertive request is not just a statement of desire, such as, "I want something to eat," or "I need help." Direct requests include a question, "May I have a piece of fruit?" or "Will you help me?" Often the question is preceded by a statement of feeling or self-disclosure, such as, "I skipped lunch today because of a ball game. May I have a piece of fruit?" or "I guess I wasn't listening well in class today. Will you help me?"

Likewise, gifted children need to know how to make straightforward refusals. Most children need to be taught that they have a right to say no to other people's *requests* (not, however, to the *demands* of teachers or parents). It is also important that children be taught to distinguish between excuses and reasons when saying no to a request. For example, suppose a child was asked to share a homework assignment. An excuse not to share this would be, "I didn't do it either." A reason for not sharing a homework assignment would be, "No, I don't believe in sharing my homework." Besides not being honest, making excuses tends to leave the door open for further requests when the situation chances. On the other hand, assertive responses shut the door on similar requests.

Children are also uncomfortable in making assertive refusals to their peers. (They are very good at making aggressive refusals, as will be shown.) A group of nine-year-olds at a school for exceptional children was asked what they would do if a friend asked to borrow their bicycle and they did not want to lend it. Only 15 percent responded with an assertive refusal. The following are some of the nonassertive ways in which the children responded to this request:

Passive:—"Loan the bicycle even though not wishing to." "Make excuses such as, 'I'm not allowed to.'" In this case, the child did not want to loan the bike, even if permitted by parents, so it is an excuse, not a reason.

Aggressive:—"Tell him he's not a good rider."

Passive-Aggressive:—"Say you'll do it and then not be home when the kid comes to pick it up."

Assertive responses, on the other hand, are direct and honest. "No, I never lend it to anybody," or "No, I'm using it this afternoon," (as long as this is the real reason for not lending it) are possible examples. Note that the latter response leaves the door open for further requesting, whereas the first statement is more final.

Refusing someone raises the possibility of that person being hurt or resentful. Thus it is important that children be taught the skill of softening a refusal. One does not have to be tactlessly blunt to get one's point across. Children need to be taught to acknowledge the other person's feelings through the use of buffering statements, such as, "I know you really want to use it, but I just don't lend it out." This kind of response does not imply that the person is backing down. It merely demonstrates that he does not wish to hurt the feelings of the requester. It must be pointed out to children that no matter how hard one tries to avoid it, occasionally a person's feelings will be hurt when his requests are denied. This is to be accepted as something natural and is not to be construed as a reason to change a refusal into an acceptance.

You can begin teaching your children assertion by both demonstrating and discussing how to make direct requests and refusals. Point out that when people want something from another, they should come right out and ask, "May I have . . . ?" or "Will you . . . ?" You will also want to point out that in the event an assertive request or refusal is ignored, the child is to calmly repeat the assertion. Emphasize that direct questions work much better than whining, hinting around, or forcing. Explain that while it is every person's right to ask for what they want, people also have the right to refuse other people's requests.

The next step is to present make-believe situations in which the child can practice assertion. Ask your children what they would do in the following situations:

A friend asks for ten cents to buy a package of potato chips. He/she did the same last week and didn't repay you. You don't want to loan the money. What do you do? What else can you do?

A boy/girl asks to crowd in front of you in the cafeteria line. You don't want to let them cut in. What do you do? What else can you do?

Your brother/sister wants to watch television and you are already watching a program and would like to see the end of it. He/she starts to change the channel. What do you do? What else can you do?

You're baby-sitting for your brother/sister; your parents have instructed you not to have a friend over. A friend wants to come over and watch TV. What do you do? What else can you do?

You're at the grocery store getting some bread for your mother. They don't have the kind your mother wanted, but the clerk gives you something like it. You don't want this kind of bread. What do you do? What else can you do?

A friend of yours is planning to play a trick on another classmate. He/she is going to (trip them, make fun of how they talk, walk, etc.) at recess. You don't want to be a part of this. What do you do? What else can you do?

The teacher accuses you of hitting a fellow student and you don't want to take the blame. What do you do? What else can you do?

When Difficult Situations Arise

Most of the shy or introverted gifted child's problems fall into one of the following three categories: 1) taking a social risk, such as trying to make friends or joining a club, 2) difficulty confronting an authority figure such as a teacher, or 3) when other children are imposing their will on the child. All of these situations can be helped by self-confidence training in the form of role play. Role play means the child practices what to say while the parent pretends to be the person the child needs to confront.

The first step in role play is to reduce the problem to a specific, well-defined goal. For instance, the child who does not like a teacher can focus the problem on asking the teacher to recognize her improved classroom behavior; or a child who is angry at friends might ask his friends not to talk behind his back. Once you are able to help the child specify the problem to a goal, you will be ready for role play.

Begin the role play by asking the child what he/she might say to start the interaction. The child should use the appropriate words that he/she would use in the real-life situation. Instead of saying, "I would tell my friends how I felt about it," the child should imagine that you are the friend and say, "I don't like it when you talk behind my back; please don't do it again." You, in turn, will want to respond as you imagine the other person would, at least to the best of your ability. An example: Dion, age nine, wanted to join the Scouts, but his friends told him it was too late and that he had already missed too much. Dion told his father about this and said he did not know what to do.

Father: What could you do about this?

Dion: Well, I dunno. I want to join, but I can't if they tell me it is too late.

Father: Do you think you could say, "That may be true, but I'd like to ask in order to find out for sure. Who should I talk to?" (Notice the suggestion is put to the child as a *question*. Throughout the role play, the parent always questions and suggests, rather than telling the child what to do.)

Dion: Yeah, that sounds good.

Father: Good. Do you think it would help if you practiced it with me to see how it goes? I could pretend to be your friend and you could ask me.

Dion: Okay, but you don't act mean, like Tommy.

Father: I'll try to act the way he would. First, just tell me what you think you want to say without acting it out.

Dion: I'm going to say, "I want to find out who I need to talk to about joining the Scouts," and if they say that it won't matter, I'll say, "That may be true, but I'd like to find out for sure."

Father: Are you ready to try that, with me being Tommy?

Dion: I want to know how to join Scouts and see if it's not too late. Who should I ask, Tommy?

Father: (as Tommy) "Well, it won't make any difference, because lot of kids want to join and you have to know stuff before they let you in."

Dion: "Yeah, but I want to ask someone anyway."

After the role play, give the child helpful feedback. For instance:

Father: Hey, that was real good. (Giving positive reinforcement for the rehearsal.) What did you like about the way you did that?

(Before proceeding to suggestions for improvement, it is important to elicit a statement of self-reinforcement for the try.)

Dion: I guess it sounded as if I wasn't scared to find out, that I just really wanted a chance to know.

Father: Right. (Reinforcing the child's self-reinforcing statement.) Was there anything you think you'd like to improve?

Dion: I don't think so.

Father: Do you think you might try it again and repeat your question, "Who do I talk to?" when you tell Tommy that you want to ask someone anyway, even if it is too late?

Dion: Didn't I do that?

Father: You did it in the first sentence, but after Tommy challenges you, it might help to ask the question again.

Dion: OK. Let's do it again.

Notice that the suggestion for improvement is phrased as a question: "Do you think it might work better if . . ." or "Would you like to try it again and this time . . ." Another example: Dave is fearful of asking questions in class, thinking he might appear stupid. This is largely because he just switched from a public to private school for gifted children.

Mother: What would you like to say to the teacher when you don't understand something—say, a math problem?
Dave: I would like to ask him to go over the solution again.
Mother: What words would you say to him?
Dave: Mr. Adams, would you go over that problem again?
Mother: Okay, now try saying that same thing over again as if you were saying it to Mr. Adams.
Dave: Mr. Adams, would you go over that problem you just explained once more?
Mother: That was really good. How did you think you did?
Dave: Pretty good.
Mother: Do you want to do it again, or do you think you can do it in class now?
Dave: I think I'd better try it once more.

Dave and his mother then rehearse the line again and keep doing so until Dave feels comfortable with the line. Each time his mother praises Dave for either doing it well or for trying, and also attempts to get Dave to say something positive about his performance.

Let us say that when Dave is asked whether he wants to try the first line again he does so, but is concerned that the teacher will not respond very positively to his questions. In this case Mother (who is playing the teacher) responds the way she anticipates Mr. Adams will.

Mother: What do you think Mr. Adams would say?

Dave: He always says things like, "You must not have been listening," or "I shouldn't have to repeat the explanation."

Mother: What do you think you could say to him then to get your point across?

Dave: I don't know.

Mother: You could restate your request by telling him, "I was listening, but I still didn't get the explanation; would you repeat it, please?" Will you try that?

Mother encourages Dave to use the broken-record technique of returning to the central issue. In addition, Dave is instructed to assertively deny that he was not listening. (Only, of course, if it is an incorrect accusation.) In addition, this example demonstrates what the parent should do if the child does not know what to say. The approach, in this case, is to make a suggestion that the child might consider, such as, "You might try . . ." or "Maybe you could . . ." These are better than statements that direct or tell the child what he should do.

Through role play and the other components of assertion training your child not only learns to be direct and honest with people, but he or she is also certain to develop a positive self-concept along the way. In addition, as well as your child, you will find yourself becoming more assertive. Perhaps best of all, assertion training will enhance your communication with your child and, therefore, will enrich the overall parent-child relationship.

Unfortunately, as previously mentioned, some gifted children will end up on the low end of the popularity totem pole. It is true that occasionally, unpopular children become stronger and more self-confident from this kind of adolescent experience. Being unpopular can force children to assess their values and worth. This assessment can cause the gifted child to conclude that what other people think is of little consequence, that what is important is what the individual thinks. Often they will develop their inner strength and resources. Such was the case of Jason, the only black student in an all-white school. His parents moved to a new area just as he was entering adolescence.

It was so hard for me at that, well, tender age. I'll admit now that I shed many private tears. I was really an outcast just when I needed to be accepted the most. It's not that the kids ever harassed me, or anything quite that overt. I think I could have dealt with that. No, instead it was a subtler, softer pressure, but one that was just as painful. I was just never included, never accepted. My parents tried to understand, tried to ease the pain. But nobody in this world can absorb the suffering of another.

My adolescence did shape my life. Because of being the only black person in an all-white world, I was forced, like many blacks, to face our beast, to question our role and our place in society. The vision of my people, and all people, arose from my adolescent experience. I am the first to admit that it has had a profound effect on my character, my strength, and therefore my life.

Jason, and others like him, are the exception rather than the rule. Most children, gifted and otherwise, who experience unpopular social standing suffer devastating repercussions. Self-esteem and self-image erode ever so slightly with each passing day, until one day there is no self-esteem left. Often these children will have difficulties relating as adults. The following two stories illustrate this point:

The day I entered a public junior high from a small private school, I knew it was going to be difficult. The fact that I was smart was held against me instead of in my favor. I was not attractive, with a huge nose (which my mother always said meant I had character), glasses, and crooked teeth. I never felt it mattered until junior high. It's funny, but I thought someday I would go from ugly duckling to beautiful swan. When I finally grew up (after it was too late), I had a nose job, my glasses replaced by contact lenses, and three years of braces! Yes, it did change my appearance, but not my self-image. I suffered so much in high school that I am even still trying to unravel the damage in therapy.

And another story:

I was never a great athlete or a good-looking guy. In our school, success with the girls depended on exactly those two factors. As a result I was so shy, so intimidated by girls, that I really can't remember talking even once to a girl until I was about twenty-one and in college. Even then it was tough. And oh, how I thought about girls; sex was always on my mind. I'm doing OK now but I don't think I'll ever be really comfortable or natural around women.

Parents can help their children before they suffer the repercussions from inadequate social skills. The first step toward this goal is to carefully assess how bad the situation is. First, discuss in great detail the child's social experiences. Ask the young adolescent questions such as, "How important do you think popularity is?" If appropriate, ask, "Why do you think you are not as popular as you would like to be?" "What do you think can be done about it?" "What incidents at school happen to you that make you feel unpopular?" Offer opinions as they present theirs.

Sometimes when a child focuses on what makes for a popular person, they are better able to understand how they might make changes for improvements. One mother tells how this worked for her daughter:

My daughter was always shy, introverted, and she preferred the company of books to that of other children. But when she entered junior high, she started wanting more friends. We talked about it and specifically, what makes a person well liked. Every day, we would discuss her observations on the subject. She was so insightful! We narrowed popularity down to three characteristics: friendliness, positive attitude, and clothes (of all things, I thought). Well, Jacklyn and I tackled each one, how a person becomes friendly and how a person demonstrates a positive attitude. Then we just made a few changes in the way she approached people and the clothes she wore and oh, her hair style. I don't think Jacklyn will ever win a popularity contest. I don't think she wants to. But now she has very close friends and seems to be doing very well socially.

Teaching Relationship Skills

If it is apparent that your gifted child has difficulty meeting boys or girls or developing pleasing relationships, a parent might ask the child whether he would like some help meeting people. If the child is willing, the parent can begin by explaining the following approach to learning basic relationship skills. Parents will want to mention that learning these relationship skills often leads to popularity. The following training program can be modified easily to meet the needs of a child of any age.

First, discuss how starting conversations with people requires true courage. Explain to the child that we are all afraid the other person won't respond nicely and that this rejection is one of the risks of initiating a conversation. Parents should also offer to practice starting conversations with the child until it is not quite so scary. Parents can reassure the child that with practice they will feel more confident about this activity.

Start by determining, with your child, appropriate questions that might lead to a conversation. Ask the child to make a list of all the possible questions he might ask the person that he is interested in getting to know. Decide with the child which are the best questions and then role play the asking of the opening questions.

Obviously, the child will play himself and the parent will pretend to be the friend. Practice until the child feels both comfortable and capable of doing it in real life.

Next, discuss how the child might initiate future contact with this person once he/she develops a rapport with the other person or once he/she notices similar interests between them. Suggest that the child close the conversation with a positive statement and a request for further contact. For instance, the child might say, "Gee, I really enjoyed talking with you. Could we exchange phone numbers? Would you care to come to my house for lunch? To see my aquarium? To go swimming?" etc. Practice the positive statement and request until the child feels comfortable. This type of role play is sure to give the child enough self-confidence to begin making friends.

PART 2—THE FAMILY ARENA

Expectations—The Problem with Being Perfect

Parents of gifted children inevitably have high expectations for their gifted children. Those expectations can be raised to dangerous heights. Some parents expect the gifted child to behave like a bright little adult; they expect dazzling scholastic performance and achievements, model behavior, and every large and small endeavor to be tackled with ease. These parents expect so much and, what's more, they are not at all surprised when the child does excel. Excellence is simply taken for granted.

The trap such parents fall into is that they are usually short on praise and big on criticism. Instead of focusing on the child's efforts to succeed, these parents develop a habit of focusing on how and where the child is falling short of their grandiose expectations. The reprimands and criticisms begin: "You could do much better," "Of course, you received an excellent report card, but why did you fall behind in social science?" "Being at the top of your class is not enough. When I was your age, I . . ." The child soon realizes that no achievement is enough. They are never able to achieve that all-important feeling of being accepted.

Most children in a "never enough" situation struggle vainly to please the unpleasable parents. They are like long-distance runners whose goal is forever being moved farther away. The faster they run, the harder they try, the more elusive their goal becomes. All because a dazzling performance is expected, taken for granted by parents. These children become praise-starved and soon find that no amount of achievement fills them with the normal sense of joy or pride.

There are many serious psychological consequences to a "never enough" syndrome. The first adverse consequence has to do with the parent-child relationship itself. In later years many of these children are unable to establish a normal adult-adult relationship with their parents. They continue to view their parents as critical, demanding people who are still not pleased. This perception is often maintained in adulthood, even when parents have earnestly abandoned the critical parent role. Too much bitterness and resentment has taken root and grown.

Sadly, many of these children seek equally critical and demanding mates as adults. In a similar fashion to what Freud called neurotic repetition, they pick mates resembling their parents in the neurotic and unconscious hope that eventually they will be able to resolve the problem. It is as though they still hope to gain the praise and acceptance they never had from their parents. Predictably, they are never able to solve the problem or even resolve feelings of low self-esteem and unacceptance from their critical, parentlike mates. One woman explains how after an unhappy ten-year marriage and a year of counseling she was able to see this pattern:

My mother was so critical and demanding that, Lord, she made an army sergeant look benevolent by comparison! I remember thinking, as a young girl, that she couldn't be my real mother, she must be the wicked stepmother in disguise. She would find fault with everything I did and said, everything from doing the dishes to the way I played the piano. Oh, and I tried to please her, how I tried. I skipped two grades and still was at the top of my class, I won awards for math and science and even poetry and, God knows, I never once got into trouble.

Of course, I picked a critical, demanding husband. I guess I was afraid I'd miss my mother. He and she would have made a delightful pair. I think he could have even found fault where my mother would be at a loss. I'm divorced now and hopefully, with the help of my therapist, I won't make the same mistake over again. But I can't tell you how badly my background has hurt me. Oh, all the depressions, frustrations, feelings of helplessness—I just hope it's over.

The "never enough" syndrome can also cause depression. Depression results from the frustration of never feeling as though one has succeeded, despite any external signs of success. Many highly successful people are unable to internalize their success, unable to actually feel that they have achieved anything. Each accomplishment leaves an empty feeling, and each accomplishment seems to erode their fragile self-esteem.

Another similar and very painful result of a parental standard of perfection is a style of behavior characterized by an immobilizing procrastination. The parent insists that, at the very minimum, the child be perfect. The adult incorporates the parent's standard of perfection; nothing less will do. Unfortunately, we live in an imperfect world; one in which perfection is an unobtainable goal. The adult can at best achieve near-perfection, but sadly, for these people, near-perfection is synonymous with failure. The knowledge of certain failure triggers procrastination in the attempt to avoid this failure. Ironically, at all times these people are aware that procrastination is also failure. And for some people, procrastination leads to complete immobilization.

As you can see, there are startling consequences to the "never enough" syndrome. Rarely are parents able to see that they are creating this situation. For this reason, the following is a program designed to enable parents to know if they are creating a "never enough" situation, followed by helpful means to change this scenario.

1. The first step is to examine an average week with your child. Consider all the things that you expect your child to accomplish without question and make a list of these items. Leave out anything that falls in the category of daily ritual—dressing for school, brushing teeth, bath, etc. However, include everything else you expect your child to do—daily homework, two hours of study, piano practice, taking out the garbage, mowing lawn, dishes, etc. Try to have a list of at least twenty items.

2. The next step is to place these items in a column. This column should be followed by three empty columns. Keep this sheet in a place that you have easy access to throughout the day.

3. Place a check mark in the first empty column every time you compliment or praise your child for doing something on the list. Place a check mark in the second empty column every time you criticize or negatively comment to your child about something on the list. At the end of a week, if no check mark has appeared in either of the first two columns, then put a check mark in the third empty column. Try to be honest in the hope that a clear, realistic picture will emerge.

4. At the end of the week, examine the columns. Add up the checks in each column. The number of checks in the first column should outweight the total of the other two columns added together. This means that you have a healthy balance between criticisms and compliments, that your children receive enough positive strokes to grow on.

If, however, the first column does not outweigh the other two columns, you might be creating a "never enough" situation. Examine which of the last two columns have the highest total. Are you being overly critical or are you taking the child's behavior for granted?

Those parents who do find that they are off balance between criticism, ignoring, and giving compliments will want to take the necessary steps to remedy the situation. The first step in solving any problem is the recognition that there is a need to change. The second step is then to start keeping a weekly chart of compliments and criticisms, along with making a conscious effort to increase compliments and decrease criticisms. This is the beginning. Maintain the list until a healthy balance can be maintained without much effort—in other words, until the compliments come easily and naturally.

The second step is to examine the nature of your compliments. There are basically two types of compliments—those that compliment an action or behavior and those that compliment the person. A balance between these two types of compliments is as essential as a balance between compliments in general and criticisms.

Most parents tend to praise children's behavior far more than they praise the children themselves. In a similar manner to the rule "Never tell a child he is bad, only that what he did was unacceptable," children need to know that they are good, worthwhile people outside of their actions. Parents are the most essential carriers of this message. Children need to know that they are both liked and loved for who they are, not for what they do. Statements that convey this message include, "You sure are a nice person to be with!" "Do you know how much joy and love you have brought your father and me?" and simply those magical three words, "I love you." Just start dropping these kinds of affectionate statements into your interaction and watch your child's face light up!

The third step is to emphasize the process instead of the outcome. This is especially important in relation to schoolwork. Instead of stressing grades or achievement, parents will want to stress the learning process that leads to grades and achievement.

Questions such as, "What did you learn?" "Are you learning from it?" "Don't you find you learn a lot from . . . ?" will all convey the importance of the learning process. These steps should really improve the parent-child relationship and help ease the problem of achieving perfection.

THE GIFTED AND THE LESS-GIFTED SIBLING

The Clyde and Farnsworth Scenario:

Once upon a time, not long ago, there was a valley. The valley was naturally divided into two parts: one part tree-lined, lush, and fertile; the other part barren, dry, and, because of the mountain shadows, darker. In this valley lived two sparrows, Clyde and Farnsworth. Clyde was strong, big, and had beautifully colored feathers, while Farnsworth was weaker, smaller, and not as prettily colored. Because of Clyde's natural superiority, he naturally chose the bright, fertile side of the valley, forcing the inferior Farnsworth to choose the dark side of the valley. Farnsworth desperately longed to live on the bright side of the valley where life was nourished and a bird's pleasure came easy. But he knew that to live there would pit him hopelessly against the superior Clyde, a competition he knew he could not win. Poor Farnsworth conceded to live on the dark side.

Unfortunately, many families have a Clyde and a Farnsworth; some even have two Clydes and a Farnsworth. The superior, gifted Clyde finds academic, recreational, and social success relatively easy and parental approval continually forthcoming. The Clydes glide effortlessly through life.

Not so for Farnsworth. He intuitively knows that he cannot

compete with Clyde in Clyde's territory. He is painfully reminded of Clyde's superiority, his own inferiority, and that what is easy for Clyde is difficult and sometimes impossible for him. Early in his life he resigns himself to living on the dark side.

Too often this is the scenario between gifted children and their less-gifted siblings. The problem can come in any form: an older gifted child and a younger, less-gifted sibling; a younger gifted child and an older, less-gifted sibling; they can be the same sex or opposite sex or they can even be twins. Very often the less-gifted child only *feels* less gifted and is, in fact, as gifted or more gifted than the sibling.

The less-gifted sibling (whether real or imagined) desperately attempts to find an unoccupied area that can provide success. Since the more-gifted child has already claimed the areas of academics, recreation (music, sports, etc.), and/or sociability, less-gifted children look elsewhere. Usually their search leads to some form of maladaptive behavior, such as becoming a discipline problem, maintaining poor scholastic performance, or even engaging in dangerous forms of delinquent and antisocial behavior. Two different parents relate their experience with the Clyde-Farnsworth scenario:

I have two daughters, Sherry, ten, and eight-year-old Diane. Sherry is a gifted child who excels in school and music. She is very conscientious about her work, which is always excellent. I am very proud of her. She is also very outgoing and popular.

Diane is the difficult child. She is so shy, rather withdrawn, and does poorly in school, even though she has as high an IQ as her sister. It seems she developed a reading problem. Her teacher says it's like stuttering when you read. She will read one line and then have to backtrack a few times to understand. This problem, even though we are trying to correct it, is causing her to fall further and further behind. And it's all psychological too; there is no physical reason for it.

We have three sons. The two oldest are considerably gifted and have made significant achievements in both sports and school. The oldest is already taking his math classes at college and he is just fifteen, while his brother has won the state championship in golf for his division. Not so hot for the youngest. I don't really know where we went wrong with him, but I sure don't remember doing anything different with him than we did with his brothers. Well, he is not quite as gifted, and he doesn't even try, anyway. He is starting to get into trouble. He is getting into an awful lot of fights and he cuts classes. We even came home once and found him drinking from our liquor cabinet. My God, the kid's only eleven, too. I don't know what we are going to do with him.

Parents often expect one child to perform at the same high standard set by another child. Sometimes in a very real sense the less-gifted child simply is not capable of meeting these expectations. These parents make the mistake of comparing one child with the other. The comparison comes in both overt and subtle forms, but each form is bound to result in one child feeling superior at the expense of the other.

The most obvious way this comparison manifests itself is through the statements or messages the parents communicate. For instance, "You know when your brother was your age . . . ," or "can you believe your sister did . . . ," or "Your sister did, so you can too." These statements will all make siblings feel like they are competing with each other.

Another manner in which a child is pitted against a sibling occurs when a parent doesn't balance the attention given between their children. Children know who the parent favors by the amount of compliments and praise or criticism and reprimands each child receives. The amount of time each child receives from the parent will also have far-reaching consequences on a child's feeling of adequacy.

Modifying the Clyde-Farnsworth Scenario

Parents who feel that a Clyde-Farnsworth scenario is being played between their children will want to take steps to balance their relationship with each child. The first place to start is to find any disparities that might exist in the way that you treat your children. Keep a chart similar to the one mentioned in the previous section, but make one for each child. Mark down any and all attention, both positive and negative, that you give to each child. Your pattern of individual interaction and the disparity of interaction between children should emerge.

Next, make certain that each child spends some amount of time alone with each parent. This will help each parent develop a positive one-on-one relationship with each child. Try to do something fun during this special time—a walk in the park or on the beach, building something together, baking a pie, swimming, playing tennis, and so forth. Furthermore, whenever possible, allow the child to choose how his alone time is spent.

Parents will also want to attempt to equalize the amount of interaction they have with each child. As previously mentioned, balancing the positive and negative statements is particularly important. Under no circumstances should parents compare siblings with each other. Instead, emphasize the differences between children, the differences that make each child a special and unique individual.

Parents might even want to pay attention to the nonverbal messages they give each child. Surprisingly, it is often only in the way a parent nonverbally reacts that any disparity can be found. Of particular importance are the nonverbals of eye contact, touching, and voice enthusiasm. Ask yourself, "Do I touch each of my children in the same manner and with the same frequency?" "Do I give each child the same amount of attention?" "Do I get more excited over one child and do I convey this?" These questions should help you balance the more subtle interactions between yourself and your children.

Perhaps most importantly, parents will want to emphasize

improvement and growth in their children instead of achievement. Don't overlook Samantha's improvement from a C average to a C+ average, even if her sister just brought home her fifth straight-A report card. Give Samantha the same amount of praise when her math test scores jump from 70 to 75 as you would her sister's perfect 100. Look for improvement and growth, no matter how small, and show each child that you noticed. Parents who just take care are certain to avoid the Clyde-Farnsworth scenario.

The Master Manipulators

Some gifted children will fall into the category of master manipulator. These children get what they want, often at great cost to a parent. The intelligence of these children allows them to assess accurately difficult situations and create a successful plan of operation to get through these situations. Undoubtedly, this is a positive trait most of the time. However, to the dismay of many parents, gifted children sometimes view parental control as the "tricky situation," one in which they must develop a plan of operation to overcome.

The gifted child's assessment usually involves finding loopholes, faults, or inconsistencies in the parent's reasoning. The plan almost always involves arguing with the parent. Some children will use other tools for manipulation: guilt induction, poignantly demonstrating their superior intelligence to the parent, and tantrums.

The problem is that the gifted child is likely to win arguments with the parents. After all, they have a vested interest and only want to do what's best. In many cases, the child is actually smarter than the parent and is able to reason better. In other cases, the child is so persistent and determined to get his way that the parent ends up giving in. One parent describes such a child:

I am a philosophy professor, pedantic by nature, and have forever preached to my two children "the power of reasoning, rational thinking, and logical consistency." Both my children are gifted, but Chris, my younger child, has used it against me. She has always been an exception—she is outgoing, popular, socially adept, rather wild and, I have to admit, smarter than I am. She really does use the very tools I gave her against me. If she ever whined, pouted, or cried, she knew I would not be swayed from my position. Instead, she knows that she must reason with me.

For instance, she wanted a motorcycle at age fourteen. As always, she had the argument well thought out. First, she presented my objections. Next, she presented why my objections were unfounded. She does this in a very calm, mature voice—much as though she was on a debating team. Then she presents all the reasons why I should allow her. She begins with the less important reasons, such as "Father, you realize that I'm in the stage of life where I am seeking more independence. A motorcycle is an excellent way of being free and independent." Those are her exact words. Then she concludes with her most powerful arguments, the statistics on motorcycle accidents of dirt riding, comparing this accident rate to other activities she engages in. Finally, she concludes with a summary of the argument! What could I do? One month later she was in the hospital with a broken leg.

What can a parent do to stop or prevent this problem? First, ackowledge that you allow yourself to be manipulated and that you're not going to take it anymore! Then you must carefully consider the issues about which you feel you are being manipulated. Divide these issues into the following three categories:

1. Issues in which the child has the total say in the matter.
2. Issues in which there is room for compromise.
3. Issues in which the child has no say in the matter.

Once your mind is made up, the rest is quite simple. Firmly refuse to argue on any issue in which the child has no choice.

State in no uncertain terms that the matter is decided and there will be no arguing. Many parents will at first find that the child still argues. In this case, repeat in a calm voice, while looking the child in the eyes, "I understand you have objections. However, the decision is made and you are not to argue with it." Be prepared to restate this as many as five times. Undoubtedly, this will be difficult in the beginning. However, once the pattern is established, you will find that you finally have control over your great master manipulator.

In summary, the first set of ingredients necessary to raise a socially healthy, gifted child are:

1. An understanding of the four most common social problems among gifted children: elitism, inadequate social skills, megalomania, and shyness.
2. Parental energy and focus on democratic and egalitarian training for the gifted child.
3. Parental energy and focus on empathy training for the gifted child.
4. Parental attention and guidance on any inadequate verbal-interaction developments in the gifted child.
5. Parental help for overcoming shyness or introversion.
6. A parental program to teach assertion skills.
7. Lots of praise, hardly any criticism.
8. Understanding the danger of a Clyde-Farnsworth scenario and avoiding this.
9. Not allowing the master manipulator to manipulate.

Chapter 5
Questions and Answers

Q: I notice that my exceptional child prefers solitary play more than other children, and I was wondering if this is normal?

A: Yes, research has shown that gifted children prefer solitary play more than other children. Gifted children are intellectually more mature than the average child; as a result, they are likely to find play with other children boring and less stimulating than solitary play. The gifted child will also tend to enjoy games that have structure at an earlier age than other children. These structured games—games with a system of rules and a definitive outcome—can usually be played alone. The gifted child seems to thrive on the challenge, the intellectual depth, and the concrete measure of success that structured games provide.

Q: My gifted teenage daughter always excelled in mathematics until she entered high school. I heard that this happens to a lot of girls. Is that true?

A: Yes. Teenage girls begin performing significantly lower than boys in mathematics once they reach high school. This is particularly disturbing considering the important role mathematical ability plays in academic and career success, especially careers in the sciences. Currently, there are many conflicting theories as to why females drop off in math abilities. Some researchers believe that it is due to socialization factors, other researchers contend that it is due to an inherent difference between the sexes, while still others believe it is due to a combination of social and genetic factors. There is no conclusive data that explains these theories one way or another.

In any case, it is important for the parents of gifted girls to encourage and support their interest in math. Be sure to explain and discuss the importance mathematics plays in our world and the girl's future career choice. Whenever possible, make the math that appears in real life (shopping, comparing value or costs, etc.) into a fun game. Some parents will want to supplement the gifted girl's math education with outside books and material and offer rewards for any extra effort the child makes in math.

Q: Won't special classes for gifted students foster elitism?

A: Segregating students based on ability could not be any worse than segregating athletes on the school's basketball team according to ability. However, no one ever seems to object to the latter practice. The truth of the matter is that all children will be separated into groups throughout their lives. Parents who do sense the gifted child becoming unduly boastful of their status will want to temper this development of elitism by incorporating the suggestions discussed in Chapter Four into their family patterns.

Q: My teenager dates boys much less intelligent than she is, and this really bothers me. Should I do something about it?

A: No. Parental criticism or interference with the people a teenager finds attractive will almost always have the opposite effect of what a well-meaning parent might intend. In other words, it often serves to strengthen the teenager's attraction. Teenage attraction to the other sex is often based on superficial characteristics, such as popularity, physical appearance, or athletic abilities. Rarely does intelligence enter this picture, let alone mutual interests, shared values, or other important relationship criteria. Fortunately for most, dating during the teen years is a far cry from marriage. Parents will certainly want to discuss the importance of other relationship criteria, such as love, mutual respect, caring, shared values and interests, etc., but this should be done in a noncritical, open atmosphere. Many parents will also find it helpful to share their own dating experiences with the teenager.

Q: My teenage son is extremely gifted and does well in school, but I'm worried because he shows no interest in the opposite sex. Do you think this is a problem?

A: That depends. Of course, we each mature and become interested in the other sex at different rates. The issue parents need to assess is whether or not the teenager is responding to a fear of dating or if he is just not ready for it. It is an important determination. Many gifted adolescents focus so much on academic and intellectual interests that they never learn to develop adequate social skills. Fear of normal social interaction is often the result. In this case, parents can learn how to help their child develop necessary social skills. Successful methods for teaching social skills are outlined in the book *Help Your Child Be Self-Confident* (Prentice-Hall, 1979).

Q: Our religion is very important to our family, but it seems that our gifted nine-year-old has already rejected it. Is there anything we can do?

A: Yes. It is common for many parents of gifted children to face this problem. It seems that the difficulty stems from the way the religion is presented to the gifted child. Very simply, the presentation is usually geared for the average child and, therefore, is not sophisticated enough to capture the precocious child's imagination. Parents faced with this problem should ask their minister, priest, or rabbi if he/she might be willing to give the child personal instruction for a period of time. We have found most religious leaders more than happy to comply with this request, for they genuinely enjoy the challenge that a gifted child often presents.

Q: I find myself objecting to many of the books my gifted child reads. While intellectually she might be able to understand them, emotionally she is not old enough. What should I do?

A: This is another common problem among parents of gifted children. We suggest that parents use the following procedure with children reading difficult or mature literature:

1. Ask the child to write a summary of the book, to allow you to assess how much of the material the child has assimilated.
2. Question what was liked and not liked about the book.
3. Discuss at length the parts of the book that might have been too difficult.

These activities will help parents buffer any difficulty the child had with the contents of the book.

Q: Can a gifted child also be learning disabled?

A: Yes, and this can have disastrous consequences. The gifted child is smart enough to compensate for the learning disability, making the disability difficult to diagnose. As the following story illustrates, this compensation often takes on monumental proportions:

"Our son was having difficulty learning to read, and the school was considering keeping him back a year in first grade. We had him tested and he had an IQ of 164! We then had his eyes checked, and that test showed he had normal vision. We were at a loss as to what to do. The strange thing was there were times when he would be able to read, but only when the teacher was asking different students to read out loud. Some time later, we learned that he was memorizing the passages that the other children read before him. In other words, the poor guy wasn't reading, he was reciting. Finally, one day my wife was talking to another mother and she suggested a near-point vision test for our son. Bingo! It turned out that while his eyes could see normally, they did not work together. He got help and is now doing fine." Parents who suspect learning difficulties will want to have complete and extensive testing administered by educational professionals. Most learning disabilities among gifted children are vision-related, so the child will need to have both visual activity and a near-point vision check administered if he/she has difficulty reading. The child can learn to read once these problems are corrected.

Appendix
A Guide to Resources for Information, Materials, and Assistance for Gifted Children

NATIONAL RESOURCES FOR THE GIFTED AND TALENTED

Office of the Gifted and Talented
U.S. Office of Education
Washington, D.C. 20202
202/962-4038

Regional Offices:

Region I: Connecticut, Maine, Massachusetts, New Hampshire, Rhode Island, Vermont

U.S. Office of Education, Region I
John F. Kennedy Federal Building
Government Center
Boston, Massachusetts 02203
617/233-5453

Region II: New Jersey, New York, Puerto Rico, Virgin Islands

U.S. Office of Education, Region II
Federal Building
26 Federal Plaza
New York, New York 10007
212/264-4370

Education for the Gifted
State Education Department
Room 314A, Main Building
Albany, New York 12224
518/474-4973

Region III: *Delaware, District of Columbia, Maryland,*
Pennsylvania, Virginia, West Virginia
U.S. Office of Education, Region III
401 North Broad Street
Philadelphia, Pennsylvania 19108
215/597-1011

Region IV: *Alabama, Florida, Georgia, Kentucky, Mississippi,*
North Carolina, South Carolina, Tennessee
U.S. Office of Education, Region IV
50 Seventh Street, N.E., Room 550
Atlanta, Georgia 20223
404/526-5311

Region V: *Illinois, Indiana, Michigan, Minnesota, Ohio, Wisconsin*
U.S. Office of Education, Region V
HEW-OE 32nd Floor
300 South Wacker Drive
Chicago, Illinois 60606
312/353-1743

Region VI: *Arkansas, Louisiana, New Mexico, Oklahoma, Texas*
U.S. Office of Education, Region VI
1114 Commerce Street
Dallas, Texas 75202
214/749-2634

Region VII: *Iowa, Kansas, Missouri, Nebraska*
Assistant Regional Commissioner
U.S. Office of Education, Region VII
Federal Office Building
601 East 12th Street
Kansas City, Missouri 64106
816/374-2528

Region VIII: *Colorado, Montana, North Dakota,*
South Dakota, Utah, Wyoming
U.S. Office of Education, Region VIII
Federal Office Building, Room 9017
1961 Stout Street
Denver, Colorado 80202
303/837-3676

Region IX: American Samoa, Arizona, California, Guam, Hawaii, Nevada, Trust Territory of the Pacific Islands
U.S. Office of Education, Region IX
Federal Office Building
50 Fulton Street
San Francisco, California 94102
415/556-3441

Region X: Alaska, Idaho, Oregon, Washington
U.S. Office of Education, Region X
Mail Stop 628
1321 Second Avenue
Seattle, Washington 98101
206/442-0450

National/State Leadership Training Institute on the Gifted and Talented
National/State Leadership Training Institute on
the Gifted and Talented
316 West Second Street, Suite 708
Los Angeles, California 90012
213/489-7470

National Clearinghouse for the Gifted and Talented
National Clearinghouse for the Gifted and Talented
The Council for Exceptional Children
1920 Association Drive
Reston, Virginia 22091
703/620-3660

The Associate for the Gifted (TAG)
The Association for the Gifted
The Council for Exceptional Children
1920 Association Drive
Reston, Virginia 22091
703/620-3660

National Association for Gifted Children
National Association for Gifted Children
Route 5, Box 630 A
Hot Springs, Arkansas 71901
501/767-2669

The Gifted Child Research Institute
The Gifted Child Research Institute
300 West 55th Street
New York, New York 10019
212/514-7059

The American Association for the Gifted
The American Association for the Gifted
15 Gramercy Park
New York, New York 10003
212/473-4266

The Council of State Directors of Programs for the Gifted
The Council of State Directors of Programs for the Gifted
Florida State Department of Education
319 Knott Building
Tallahassee, Florida 32304
904/599-5807

STATE RESOURCES FOR THE GIFTED AND TALENTED

State programs vary considerably in their ability to provide service to the gifted and talented. The states included in the list were chosen for their ability to provide multiple services.

Northern California
Consultant for Mentally Gifted
California State Department of Education
721 Capitol Mall
Sacramento, California 95814
916/445-4036

Southern California
Consultant for Mentally Gifted
California State Department of Education
214 West First Street, Room 803-A
Los Angeles, California 90012
213/620-4224

Connecticut
Consultant for Gifted and Talented
Connecticut State Department of Education
P.O. Box 2219
Hartford, Connecticut 06115
203/566-2492

California Parents for the Gifted
5521 Reseda Boulevard, Suite 10
Tarzana, California 91356
213/345-1356

Connecticut Association for the Gifted
Southern Connecticut State College
New Haven, Connecticut 06515
203/397-2101

Florida Association for the Gifted
University of Southern Florida
Special Education
Tampa, Florida 33620
813/974-2100

Georgia Association for Gifted Education
P.O. Box 557
Alamo, Georgia 30411

Massachusetts Commission on the Academically Talented
Brockton Public Schools
Brockton, Massachusetts 02402
617/588-7800

Michigan Association for the Academically Talented, Inc.
517 Chamberlain Street
Flushing, Michigan 48433
313/659-5126

Minnesota Council for the Gifted
4567 Gaywood Drive
Minnetonka, Minnesota 55331
612/935-8055

Nebraska Association for the Gifted
Lincoln Public Schools
Administration Building
Lincoln, Nebraska 68508
402/475-1081, Ext. 273

The Gifted Child Society, Inc.
59 Glen Gray Road
Oakland, New Jersey 07436
201/337-7058

Ohio Association for the Gifted
2320 McKinley Avenue

Lakewood, Ohio 44107
216/226-0610

Pennsylvania Association for the Study
and Education of the Mentally Gifted
Wilkes College
Wilkes-Barre, Pennsylvania 18703
717/824-4651, Ext. 279

Texas Association for the Education of the Gifted
P.O. Box 547
Austin, Texas 78767
512/472-4963

State Advisory Committee for the Gifted and Talented
Old Capitol Building
Olympia, Washington 98504
206/753-3222

GIFTED AND TALENTED CONSULTANTS—
STATE EDUCATION AGENCIES

Alabama

Cynthia R. Aguero, Cons.
Program for Exceptional Children & Youth
868 State Office Building
Montgomery, AL 36130
205/832-3230

Alaska

Diane LeResche, Cons.
Office for Exceptional Education
Pouch F, State Department of Education
Juneau, AK 99811
907/465-2970

American Samoa

Dennis McCray, Prog. Dir.
Department of Special Education
Pago Pago, American Samoa 96799
Overseas Operator 2435

Arizona

Randy Eubank, Coordinator
Division of Special Education
535 W. Jefferson
Phoenix, AZ 85007
602/255-5009

Arkansas

Clifford Curl, Cons.
Special Education Section
Division of Instructional Services
Arch Ford Educational Building
Little Rock, AR 72201
501/371-2161

California

Elinor McKinney, Mgr., G/T Ed.
California State Department of Education
721 Capitol Mall
Sacramento, CA 95814
916/322-5954

Dr. Paul Plowman, Admin. Cons.
Jack Mosier, Admin. Cons.
Gifted & Talented Education
California State Department of Education
721 Capitol Mall
Sacramento, CA 95814
916/322-5954

Colorado

Gerald Villars, Cons.
G/T Student Prog. Co. Dept. of Education
State Office Building, 201 E. Colfax
Denver, CO 80203
303/892-2111

Connecticut

Wm. G. Vassar, Cons.
State Department of Education
P. O. Box 2219
Hartford, CT 06115
203/566-3444

Delaware

Thomas Pledgie, Supervisor
Program of Exceptional Children
State Department of Public Instruction
Townsend Building
Dover, DE 19901
302/678-4667

District of Columbia

Patsy Baker Blackshear
Seaton Elementary School
10th &. Rhode Island Ave., N.W.
Washington, D.C. 20001
202/673-7054

Florida

Joyce Runyon, Cons., Program for G/T
Dept. of Education, Bur. of Ed. for Exceptional Students
Clemons Building A
Tallahassee, FL 32301
904/488-3103

Georgia

Margaret Bynum, Cons. G/T
State Office Building
Atlanta, GA 30334
404/565-2414

Guam

Victoria T. Harper, Assoc. Supt.
Special Education, Department of Education
P. O. Box DE
Agana, Guam 96910
Overseas Operator 772-8418

Hawaii

Pearl Ching, Prog. Spec.
State Department of Education
1270 Queen Emma Street, Room 1206
Honolulu, HI 96813
808/548-2474

Idaho

Genelle Christensen, Coord.
State Department of Education
Len B. Jordan Office Building
650 W. State
Boise, ID 83720
208/384-3940

Illinois

Thomas Ward, Dir., Prog. for Gifted
State Department of Education
100 N. First Street
Springfield, IL 62777
217/782-3810

Indiana

Arlene Manager, Cons. G/T Ed.
Division of Curriculum
Capitol Building, Room 229
Indianapolis, IN 46204
317/927-0111

Iowa

Shirley Perkins, Cons.
Grimes State Office Building
E. Fourteenth & Grand Avenue
Des Moines, IA 50319
515/281-3264

Kansas

Elwood Houseman, Director
Special Education Admin., State Dept. of Education
120 E. Tenth Street
Topeka, KS 66612
913/296-3866

Kentucky

Susan Leib, Prog. Mgr., Gifted Education
State Department of Education
1809 Capitol Plaza Tower
Frankfort, KY 40601
502/564-4774

Louisiana

Ruth Castille, Sect. Chief
Theresa Richardson & Dean Frost, Coords.
Program for Gifted
State Department of Education
Capitol State, P.O. Box 44064
Baton Rouge, LA 70804
504/342-3636

Maine

Patricia O'Connell
Division of Special Education
State Dept. of Education & Cult. Services
Augusta, ME 04333
207/289-3451

Maryland

Lynn Cole & Janice Wickless, Cons.
State Department of Education
200 W. Baltimore
Baltimore, MD 21201
301/659-2312

Massachusetts

Roselyn Frank, Bur. of Student Serv.
State Department of Education
31 St. James Ave., Room 532
Boston, MA 02116
617/727-5756

Michigan

Nancy Mincemoyer, Cons.
General Ed. Serv., State Department of Education
P.O. Box 30008
Lansing, MI 48909
517/373-8793

Minnesota

Lorraine Hertz, Coord.
Gifted Ed., Div. of Instruction
State Department of Education
641 Capitol Square
St. Paul, MN 55101
612/296-4072

Mississippi

Betty Walker, Division of Instruction
State Department of Education
P.O. Box 771
Jackson, MS 39205
601/354-6950

Missouri

Nell Sanders, Dir., Gifted & Alternative Prog.
State Department of Education
Jefferson Building, Box 480
Jefferson City, Missouri 65102
314/751-2453

Montana

Nancy Lukenbill, Cons.
Office of Public Instruction
Helena, MT 59601
406/449-3116

Nebraska

Anne B. Crabbe, Supervisor
Prog. for Gifted, State Department of Education
301 Centennial Mall S.
Lincoln, NE 68509
402/471-2446

Nevada

Jane Early, Cons.
Nevada Department of Education
400 W. King Street
Carson City, NV 89710
702/885-5700, Ext. 214

New Hampshire

Trina Osher, Cons.
Special Education, Department of Education
64 N. Main Street
Concord, NH 03301
603/271-3741

New Jersey

Ted Gourley, Cons.
State Department of Education

225 W. State Street
Trenton, NJ 08625
609/292-8412

New Mexico
F. Gutierrez, Dir., Spec. Ed.
Department of Education, Education Building
Santa Fe, NM 87503
505/827-2793

New York
Roger W. Ming, Supervisor
State Department of Education for Gifted
Albany, NY 12234
518/474-4973

North Carolina
Division of Exceptional Children
State Department of Public Instruction
Raleigh, NC 27611
919/733-3004

Ruby Murchison, Cons.
P.O. Box 786
Carthage, NC 28327
919/947-5871

North Dakota
LaDonna Whitmore, Coord.
Department of Public Instruction
Division of Special Education
State Capitol
Bismarck, ND 58505
701/224-2277 or 2247

Ohio
George Fichter, Cons.
Ohio Department of Education
933 High Street
Worthington, Ohio 43085
614/466-8854

Oklahoma

Renee Amonson
State Department of Education, Hodge Building
2500 N. Lincoln
Oklahoma City, OK 73105
405/521-3353

Oregon

Robert J. Siewert, Spec.
State Department of Education
700 Pringle Parkway, S.E.
Salem, OR 97310
503/378-8460

Pennsylvania

Jean G. Farr, Supervisor, Prog. for GT
333 Market Street
Harrisburg, PA 17108
717/783-6887

Bureau of Special Education, State Dept. of Education
P.O. Box 911
Harrisburg, PA 17126

Puerto Rico

Esther Pedroza-Gabriel, Title I Coord.
Office of External Resources
Department of Education
Hata Rey, Puerto Rico 00924
809/765-1475

Rhode Island

Judy Edsal, Cons., Prog. for GT
State Department of Education
227 Promenade Street
Providence, RI 02908
401/277-2821

South Carolina

Cons., Prog. for the Gifted
State Department of Education
803 Rutledge Building
1429 Senate Street
Columbia, SC 29201
803/758-2652

South Dakota
Robert R. Geigle, Cons.
Section for Special Education
Kneip Building
Pierre, SD 57501
605/773-3678

Tennessee
Barbara Russell
116 Cordell Hull Building
Nashville, TN 31219
615/741-1896

Texas
Ann G. Shaw, Director G/T
Texas Education Agency
201 E. Eleventh Street
Austin, TX 78746
512/475-6582

Trust Territory
Carol Shulkind, Director
Leadership Training Center for G/T
Ebeye, Marshall Islands
P.O. Box 1748
APO San Francisco, CA 96555

Utah
Jewel Bindrup, GT Cons.
Utah Board of Education
250 E. Fifth South
Salt Lake City, UT 84111
801/533-6040

Vermont
Dr. Karlene Russell, Director
Special Education, State Department of Education
Montpelier, VT 05602
802/828-3141

Virginia
> Dr. Joseph White, Director, Spec. Prog. for GT,
> State Department of Education
> P.O. Box 6-A
> Richmond, VA 23216
> 804/770-3317

Virgin Islands
> Robert Rogers, State Director of Special Education
> Department of Education, Box 630, Charlotte Amalie
> St. Thomas, VI 00801
> 809/774-0100, ext. 217

Washington
> June Lee Peek, Director G/T
> Department of Public Instruction
> Old Capitol Building
> Olympia, WA 98504
> 206/753-1140

West Virginia
> Barbara Jones, Division of Special Education
> Department of Education, Bldg. B., Unit 6
> Room 337B, Capitol Complex
> Charleston, WV 25305
> 304/348-2034

Wisconsin
> Thomas F. Diener, Supervisor, GT
> Department of Public Instruction
> 125 S. Webster Street
> Madison, WI 53702
> 608/266-2658

Wyoming
> Sue Holt, Coord., Language Arts & Gifted Ed.
> State Department of Education, Hathaway Building
> Cheyenne, WY 82002
> 307/777-7411

Index